Reverend Be........s
Dream for Appalachia

by
Reverend Ralph W. Beiting

with
Tom Pelletier

Cover photo by Jeff Rogers
Inset photo by Lorraine Corsale

TABLE OF CONTENTS

This book is dedicated to the people all over America who make dreams come true for the poor of Appalachia by supporting the Christian Appalachian Project.

The Christian Appalachian Project
1964-1992

For more than 40 years, Fr. Ralph W. Beiting has worked to ease the pain caused by poverty among the people of Appalachia. More than 25 years ago he founded an inter-denominational Christian organization called the Christian Appalachian Project (CAP). By offering long-term, self-help solutions to the problems that hold Appalachia's people back, CAP gives the poor a chance to work themselves out of poverty.

CAP provides educational programs, home repair assistance, business-development programs, and visitation programs for the elderly as well as emergency relief and more. With nearly seventy programs and activities, CAP brings happiness and peace to those in need.

Through the generous work of thousands of volunteers, hundreds of local workers and a host of loyal donors from all over the country, CAP has become one of the largest relief organizations in America.

PROLOGUE—
Dreams and Mustard Seeds

When the disciples came to Jesus and asked Him why they couldn't do the things He did, He said to them, "Amen, I say to you, if you have faith the size of a mustard seed, you will say to this mountain, 'Move from here to there,' and it will move. Nothing will be impossible for you." (Matthew 17:20)

Sometimes when I see the continuing poverty and pockets of despair in Appalachia, I feel the disciples' frustration. I wish I had Jesus' power to heal the hurt, and open the eyes of the blind.

That's when I have to remind myself that Jesus said I do have the power to move mountains. Jesus called that power faith, but He might just as well have called that power "dreams" for faith and dreams are tightly intertwined.

Jesus could have said, "If you have a dream the size of a mustard seed, you will say to this mountain, 'Move from here to there,' and it will move. Nothing will be impossible for you."

When I was first appointed pastor of a small parish in Lancaster, Kentucky in 1950, people often came to my house seeking help. "My children are hungry," they'd say, or "I don't have any winter clothes for my babies."

I don't know why they came to me. Whatever made them think a Catholic priest would have baby clothes lying around? But they did come to me and I remember praying in bed at night, wishing—dreaming—that I could help them.

That tiny dream that I could help the families knocking on my door, was the mustard seed from which the Christian Appalachian Project grew.

I went home to where I had grown up in Northern Kentucky, on the Ohio border. I asked my parents, and my brothers and sisters, and every person I knew, if they had extra food, or clothes, or a few dollars they could spare for the poor of Appalachia. I told them I had a dream to help those who'd been ignored by America's prosperity.

My friends responded, and I returned to my church with a carload of food and clothes. I zigzagged a few ropes across the big trees in front of the church and each Saturday I put out the clothes with a large sign that said "FREE CLOTHES."

At first, we gave everything away. It wasn't long before I realized this wasn't really in the best interest of the people in the greatest need. Certain people abused this generosity. They came early, picked out all the best things and hauled them off. The next week, I'd see them down the road, having a little yard sale, selling the things they'd been given for nothing.

There was a much larger group of people who refused to come, even though they were in great need, because they had too much dignity and pride to accept a handout. The last thing I wanted to do was squash that pride in self-reliance. There had to be another way.

We began charging for the clothes. The prices were almost insignificant, but they allowed people to keep their dignity. Of course, we waived even the small charges for families who had been burned out of their homes, or fallen victim to some other emergency.

Over the months and years, the Saturday morning sales expanded. First it was clothes, then pots and pans, then blankets and sheets, then used furniture, until we had a regular second-hand department store. The dream was sprouting.

One of our problems was to find a place to sort and store items until the seasons came around again. At the end of summer, we got summer things; at the end of winter, we got winter things. Also, the front lawn of the church was usually a pleasant place for a sale, but sometimes it rained, or was too hot. When we built a new church behind those big maple trees, the basement became our first store . . . and the dream grew a little bigger.

Eventually the basement was too small so we rented a store uptown. That one store became two, and then three . . . and the dream grew even more.

As our "Attic Stores," as we called them, multiplied, I insisted that we not treat our visitors like clients or customers. They weren't second-class citizens coming for a handout. We considered them our friends. I insisted we display the clothes pleasantly. We didn't just pile them up on a table, but hung them on racks and displayed them just like a department store. Our visitors were treated with great respect and courtesy—as if they had all the money in the world. It wasn't money that made them important, it was the fact that they were our friends.

That was the beginning of a new dream—the dream that we could become friends to those who desperately needed, most of all, a good friend.

Soon, the Attic Stores became more than just retail establishments, they became social places. Some women came every day. They went through the motions of shopping, but it was clear that mostly they were looking for someone to talk to. Of all the problems of Appalachia, the simple isolation of a rural mountain existence, cut off from mainstream American life, may be the most crippling. We human beings are very social creatures. Without friends we cannot thrive.

Of course, as friends, we became privy to the problems of life in Appalachia. One woman's husband had just been laid off, and couldn't find another job. Another family had been burned out of their old trailer, and didn't have any insurance money to buy a new one. From those needs grew new dreams of job programs, emergency assistance programs, and more.

The small amounts we charged at our Attic Stores added up over time and helped fund these other programs. One small dream was leading to more dreams, bigger dreams.

The dream was now growing and branching rapidly—putting out new mustard seeds.

Each tiny seed, each little dream, must be nurtured. It must be watered and fed. Sometimes we're so involved in the day-to-day tasks of our work that we forget the dreams behind the work.

This is not only true of CAP, but it's probably true in your own life as well. We should all take a few minutes each day to think and pray about our dreams to keep them from withering away.

That's why I wrote this book. I want to make sure that we at CAP, and our supporters across the country, don't lose sight of our dreams.

In each of the following chapters, I will tell you about a dream that led to one of CAP's programs. I hope to show you how those programs help the dreams of Appalachia's poorest people come true. Some of the people you'll meet here are friends of mine, some of them I know through CAP volunteers and employees.

At the end of each chapter, I hope I can inspire you with a new dream of what CAP can still do to improve and grow to help make Appalachia whole again.

You probably dream that your life might make the world a little better place. If that's true, I hope this book will convince you that your support for the Christian Appalachian Project, as a donor, a volunteer, or through prayer, can be a way to make that dream come true.

God has dreams too. His dream is that we will "love our neighbors as ourselves." When our dreams mesh with God's dream for us, we cannot fail. Jesus said, "Ask and you will receive; seek and you will find; knock and the door will be opened to you." (Luke 11:9) He said we could tell the mountains to move and they'd move.

I love the mountains of Appalachia and I want them to stay right where they are. But I do have dreams for this beautiful land. I hope, in writing this book, I can inspire you with those dreams, and gain your help to make them come true.

I don't want to move the mountains, but with the help of my friends all over the country, I want to move the people of Appalachia to a new life of faith and health and prosperity. I want to bring them friendship and God's love.

I want them to dream again.

Dreams for the Children

. . . where children are cherished, nurtured, and shown the simple wonders of God's creation . . .

Jesus said we could move mountains. I know this is true, but I've found it's much easier to move the foothills that will someday grow into mountains, than it is to move the mountains themselves.

That's why most of my dreams for Appalachia focus on the children. Adults often resist attempts to change their lives. In fact, I know that, as much as I try to be open to the wisdom of others, there is a part of me that resists "advice."

Children on the other hand, thank God, are much more open to follow a new example. It's a whole lot easier to move a foothill than a mountain.

This was painfully obvious to us when we ran our first rummage stores. We tried to convince the adults who came to us that there were healthier ways to live. That there was great value in education. That there was hope.

They listened politely, and often even agreed . . . and then went on living as they always had.

I guess we weren't ready to tackle the mountains

yet. But we dreamed we could reach the children. We began holding story hours at our rummage stores. Once or twice a week, volunteers would gather a group of children and read to them, trying to instill in them the love of reading, and show them new possibilities for their lives.

The kids enjoyed the story hours tremendously, and their parents got the first inkling of what education could mean to their kids. Another small dream had taken root.

The story hours were nice, but what if we could spend more time with the kids? What if we could separate them from poverty and despair, just for a little while, and breathe new life, new enthusiasm and new hope into them?

From that questioning came the dream of a summer camp for Appalachia's poorest children. At the time it seemed a pipe dream. I couldn't imagine where we'd get the money to build a summer camp, but I continued to dream about it.

The more faith I had, and the more I dreamed, the more possible the impossible became.

I began writing to folks all over the country, explaining my dreams for Appalachia's children, and I was pleasantly surprised at the generosity of people who lived hundreds and even thousands of miles from Appalachia. I was afraid that people in California wouldn't care about little children in the hills of Kentucky, but they did. Generosity is one of America's unifying principles, and one of her great beauties.

Using that support, and proceeds from our rummage stores, we bought a plot of land on Herrington Lake in Lancaster, KY. Then we bought a second plot, and a third, until we had room to build cabins and create a summer camp that could handle about 55 kids at a time.

Our dream was that at our camps, children would meet other children from other counties. We hoped they'd learn from each other and grow together to build a new Appalachian society that could triumph over poverty. We also hoped to bring black and white children together, something that simply did not happen in Appalachia in the 1950s. Little by little, those dreams came true.

Today, CAP has two summer camps and holds Bible camps and day camps throughout the summer. More than 600 of Appalachia's poorest children attend these camps each summer. What this means to the children is best told by their own stories.

*****

The Terror of Camp Shawnee

Michael was one of those kids who make camp counselors want to quit. He was a smart aleck, a disruptive force in every activity and he resisted every attempt to correct his behavior. Jane, his camp counselor, tried to reach out to him and find out what made him so angry, but he wouldn't even look at her. Finally, in near desperation, we moved him into another group with a different counselor. I'm sure Jane heaved a large sigh of relief—Michael was someone else's problem now.

He was Jim's problem.

At first Michael was just as disruptive in Jim's group, but Jim didn't give up on him. Little by little he cracked the wall of aggression that Michael used to protect himself. One day, the wall collapsed.

Jim found Michael in tears. When he asked the boy what the matter was, the growing trust between them allowed Michael to finally open up. He told Jim that his little sister was very sick. His parents were terribly worried and stressed over her condition. Consequently they hadn't had the time or energy to meet Michael's needs.

Poor Michael was torn between worry over his sister, whom he loved dearly, and feelings of abandonment and self-pity. Originally he had looked forward to coming to camp. Now he felt it was just one more separation, one more burden for him to carry. It was just too much for those little eight-year-old shoulders.

Once Jim understood why Michael was so upset, their relationship blossomed. What Michael needed most was a friend—an adult who could show him that he was wanted, understood, and cared for.

Jim fit the bill perfectly.

Almost instantly, Michael's disruptive behavior stopped. He became helpful and courteous to counselors and the other children. In fact, by the end of camp, Michael was awarded the "Outstanding Camper Award." Quite a turnaround for the "Terror of Camp Shawnee."

That camp session was only one short week in Michael's life, but I can't help but feel that the experience will color the rest of his days. Because of isolation and poverty, many of the Appalachian poor—especially the kids—have no one to turn to in crisis. Often the only comfort available comes from a bottle, and you'd be amazed at how early an age some children turn to the short-lived and doubled-edged comfort that comes from alcohol or drugs.

That summer, Michael learned that he was not alone. He was a valuable person and others would care about him and help him when the chips were down. I don't think he'll forget that anytime soon. It's my dream that our camps will help teach that lesson to all of Appalachia's children.

The Giant Suitcase

Most of our kids show up at camp with a few items of clothing stuffed into a paper bag. Steve had a huge suitcase. At first the camp counselors wondered why he'd brought so many clothes. Then they wondered how such a little boy could carry such a large suitcase. Their curiosity got the better of them and they asked Steve to show them what he'd brought. "I don't want to open it right now," he told them.

When Steve was settled in his cabin with the other children, Keith asked him again to let him see what he'd brought. He resisted, but Keith was persistent, and when he and Steve were alone, he finally agreed to open the mysterious suitcase.

The suitcase was completely empty.

One of the most painful aspects of the poverty that pervades these hills is shame. The people of Appalachia know how much wealth other Americans have. They see the cars, the beautiful houses—the designer clothes—and it hurts.

Having been raised in the Great Depression, I remember that feeling. To admit you are poor makes you feel small, insignificant, a failure. In the abstract, we all agree that what you own doesn't determine your worth. But that ideal is usually upheld most strongly by those who aren't poor. It's hard to feel equal when your shoes have holes in them and your clothes are tattered.

Steve was ashamed to admit the clothes on his back were all he owned. I can imagine the pain his mother felt as well, when she sent him off to camp knowing he might be shamed for being poor.

Of course, we do stress very strongly to the kids,

and to adults as well, that poverty is not a crime, and that not having money doesn't mean you don't have worth. At the same time, we work in all our programs to help the people of Appalachia find prosperity and self-respect.

My dream is that we can teach the children that their worth is not determined by their wealth, but also that they can work towards a future free from poverty.

Fireworks and Disappointment

At camp, we try to expose the children to things they've never seen or done before. We want to show them that, ''the world is their oyster.'' Appalachian kids grow up thinking ''the holler is their oyster.''

Sometimes we do that by teaching a child to swim, row a boat, or tie a knot. Other times we try to show them the simple pleasures and entertainments other Americans take for granted. One year, during one of the boys' weeks at Camp Shawnee, we decided to surprise the 9, 10, and 11 year old boys by taking them to the fireworks on the Fourth of July. Many of the boys had never seen fireworks before, and when the surprise leaked out, the news spread like wildfire through the camp, becoming, as often happens with rumors, embellished as it went.

Al, the camp's director was startled when nine

year old Victor came to him, "I heard there was going to be a surprise after the fireworks . . . what is it?"

Al was taken aback for a second. The fireworks were the surprise, nothing was planned for afterwards. But Victor insisted that all the boys in camp were talking about the exciting event that would take place after the fireworks.

Al probably should have squashed the boys' excitement right there, but he just couldn't do it, "These kids have seen so much disappointment all their lives, I just couldn't bring myself to knock them down one more time."

So instead, Al made a few phone calls and convinced a local ice cream shop to stay open late, and be prepared to serve 85 ice cream cones to the boys of Camp Shawnee.

Those kids still talk about that night. The police saved front row spots for us at the park where the fireworks were held, and the kids sat on blankets and marveled at the explosive show being played across the sky. When the show was over, it was quite late, but we tramped 85 tired young boys into the ice cream store.

The boys were in such awe of all the attention that they behaved like angels. There was nary a peep while they politely ate their ice cream. If you've had even three young boys in a room at once, you know how remarkable this was.

One of my dreams for Appalachia's children is

that they'll be treated more like the precious little angels God meant them to be. I dream of a day when the world truly is their oyster and they are loved by all the adults around them. It wasn't entirely by plan, but on that one Fourth of July night, I believe we came close to showing those boys such a dream.

*****

As well as our summer camps have worked out, my dream is still unfulfilled. We must create another three or four camps at least, and find more volunteer camp counselors to staff them during the summer. Until then, the dream that Appalachia will be a place where all children are cherished, nurtured, and shown the simple wonders of God's creation can't come true.

When we first started our summer camps, I often sat at the campfire at night, with all the children gathered around me and the fire crackling. I'll never forget those nights. I told the children ghost stories, stories about wild animals or stories of Daniel Boone and the other heroes of Appalachia's past.

Eventually, the kids began to get sleepy, and the dying fire allowed the star-twinkling night sky to descend. At that point, I always made sure to ask the children about their dreams. Usually they looked at me blankly. In those days, Appalachia's poorest children were not generally brought up to dream. Life was hard work, little joy, and lots of pain. When I asked them to dream, they hardly understood what I meant.

So I told them my dreams. I told them that I could imagine them as doctors, businessmen, scientists, or ministers or priests. I could imagine Appalachia as it would be when they grew up, bright and strong—America's pride and joy.

Little by little the children got the idea, and began to dream themselves. The ability and desire to dream is so inborn in us— a reflection of the Almighty, I'm convinced—that even though these children had never had the opportunity to dream before, they took to it immediately.

I still sit around campfires with our children today, and I still ask them to dream. I love those dreams . . . they hold the promise and the future of Appalachia.

Dreams of the Parents

*. . . where children reach their God-given
potential and face a future bright with promise . . .*

Once our summer camp was operating, I had
a crazy dream that we could open a preschool for
the children of the poor in Appalachia.

To realize how crazy this dream was, you have
to remember that at that time, the nationwide Head
Start program had not even been proposed, and
no one had ever put together a preschool specifically to help the children of poverty overcome the
limitations that being poor places on them.

I've always believed that education begins long
before first grade or even kindergarten. It starts
the day a child is born.

If we opened a preschool to help Appalachia's
poor children, we could help them enter first grade
with the same skills as middle-class children. To
create such a preschool program, we had to im-
itate the Appalachian pioneers of old, and innovate
as we went along.

Of course, we had to win the approval of
parents—not an easy task. Generations of poverty
in Appalachia had killed the dreams of parents.

Many parents didn't believe in, or even understand, the value of education. The only future for girls was to get married and become mothers. The only future for boys was to work in the coal mines. A college degree, or even a high school diploma, is of little use in the back-breaking work of coal mining.

On top of that, to admit that their children needed educational help, Appalachian parents, many of whom are illiterate, had to admit that their own education was deficient. They had to concede that they weren't necessarily the best role models for their children. You can imagine how hard that was.

Appalachian parents love their children dearly. Like parents everywhere, they want the best for their children. But in the face of poverty, it often seems to parents that the best thing for a child to do is find a job, any job, as quickly as possible —even if it means dropping out of school, or working in a job with no future. Any job is better than living on welfare.

But dreams are highly contagious—and children are the best carriers. The kids who spent time at our summer camps and Bible schools went home and promptly infected their parents with visions of a better life.

Parents began to dream that their children could escape poverty if only they could get a good education. With the coal mines hiring fewer and fewer workers, and coal-related industries suffering as well, parents realized that the old ways wouldn't work for their children.

I have no doubt that the idea to create preschools for Appalachia's poorest children would have failed miserably if outsiders had tried it. But because of our Attic Stores and summer camps—because those earlier dreams came true—many parents began to feel that CAP was not just a social service agency, we were family—and family is everything in these hills.

When we talked to parents about sending their kids to our new preschool, many of them surprised us by agreeing. I know it wasn't easy for them. I can still see the doubt and insecurity of those parents—our first parental dreamers.

Every morning as our van picked up their children for preschool, mothers would go through agony. They were not used to letting their three-year-olds and four-year-olds out of their sight. One of the results of poverty is a feeling of paranoia about the outside world. When you are at the bottom of the ladder, it's not hard to imagine that those above you will step on you.

The parents of our first students had a lot of courage and faith. A dream can do that to you.

In those early days, our preschools, which we came to call child development centers, were housed in church halls and rented office space. Eventually we built schools specifically to meet the needs of small children.

The dream was moving and taking shape.

In the very beginning, we decided parents should help out at our preschools instead of paying tuition. Each mother or father was required to work two days at the school per month. This not only provided some of the labor needed, but also helped parents learn valuable educational and parenting skills they could use at home.

Those first preschools were an instant success. We learned a great deal as we went along, but right off the bat we knew we were on the right track— we knew this dream was good.

When the children who had been through our child development centers entered first grade, we heard report after report about how well adjusted to school life they were, how sharp and interested they were, how they had an appetite for learning.

Today, thanks to the generosity of our supporters, we have five child development centers working with over 600 Appalachian children and parents. Our staff and volunteers are dedicated and inspired by the dream. Though that dream is not yet complete, I think our preschool child development program is as good as any in the country.

*****

Timmy's Protector

When Timmy first came to our child development center he was a child of extremes. He had been neglected as a baby, and though he appeared to have recovered, sometimes it seemed as if he just had to act out his pain and frustration. One minute he would be quiet and angelic while listening to his teacher read a story. Not five minutes later he could be violent and abusive.

But he was the world's best big brother.

When his little three-year-old sister Lisa began attending the school, Timmy changed. Lisa was small, quiet and shy, and Timmy felt he had to protect her and look out for her.

He held her hand when they walked into school. He showed her to the bathroom and the lunchroom. He tenderly guided her through each day, and when Lisa was around, Timmy was never violent or angry.

Then one day he made a rude remark to his teacher and rather than wait for the discussion he knew would follow, he ran out the door and into the playground. His teacher followed, but she lost sight of him. When she found him in one corner of the yard, his sister was there with him. Lisa stood in front of Timmy with her arms outstretched as if to hide and guard him.

She planted her feet and glared at the teacher with her big blue eyes. Her expression said, "You leave my brother alone!"

Timmy's teacher was so touched by Lisa's loyalty and courage that she didn't know whether to laugh or cry.

Lisa's defense of Timmy that day may have been misplaced, but we all need a friend like that who will stick by us through thick and thin.

One of my dreams is that CAP can be that kind of friend to Appalachia's children. We need to stick up for them and make sure they get the help they need and deserve. We need to face their problems with courage and determination. We need to plant our feet and spread our arms and be there when they need us.

The Education Salesman

Hank's mother Ivey was desperate for us to find a place for him at our child development center. Hank had been taken away from Ivey for neglect. A judge later agreed to let Hank go home, but only if Ivey enrolled him in a preschool program.

Our first visit to Hank's house was quite an adventure. To get to his house you have to throw caution to the wind and plunge down a gravel road that leads deeper and deeper into a dark forest. After many miles you finally come to a clearing where a few houses stand. You can't miss Hank's house. It's a beat up old shack in a desolate yard where a few brave tufts of grass struggle to survive in the dirt and dust.

Hank was filthy and so was the house. It seemed that Ivey hadn't learned much from Hank's forced separation. Sometimes though, what looks like neglect is really ignorance. Ivey had left school at 13, and had never had a good role model. She grew up in dirt and poverty, and she lived that way herself. But she was eager to learn. On our second visit, Hank was squeaky clean.

Because of the distance and the treacherous road to Hank's house, we decided we couldn't send the child development center van out every day to pick him up. It would take too long, and hold up the other kids from school. But we couldn't just ignore Hank's plight. We take great pride at CAP in our ability to be flexible. Many other programs would just have said, "Sorry, you don't fit our schedule. Good luck somewhere else."

CAP is family, however, and when you're family, you don't just go by the book, you bend and twist to make things work. Instead of bringing Hank to our preschool, we brought preschool to Hank.

We recruited Linda, one of our volunteers, to drive to Hank's house and teach him at home. She discovered that Hank was a bright child, but he was significantly behind in many areas. With her help, he made rapid progress over the weeks and months, and seemed to really enjoy learning.

Linda also worked with Ivey. She gently suggested new ideas about parenting. Little by little, Ivey became more involved in Hank's school work and play.

When summer came and school officially ended,

Linda continued to visit, and she learned that Hank had been busy selling the joy of education. First Hank's older sisters, home from school, wanted to join in. Then Hank's cousins. Then some neighborhood kids. Sometimes there would be ten kids crowded into Ivey's tiny living room.

There are hundreds of salesmen like Hank all over these hills now. Every child who goes through our child development center tells the other kids how much fun it is, and their parents tell other parents how much their kids learn. Teachers who have our children in first and second grades tell parents with younger children. Every year, the demand grows . . . the dream grows.

*****

Through our child development centers we have awakened the dreams of Appalachia's parents. More and more they realize that education can be a path to success and happiness for their children.

As the book of Proverbs says:

Happy the man who finds wisdom,
  the man who gains understanding!
For her profit is better than profit in
  silver, and better than gold is her
  revenue;

She is more precious than corals,
  and none of your choice possessions can
  compare with her.
Long life is in her right hand,
  in her left are riches and honor;
Her ways are pleasant ways,
  and all her paths are peace.

                                    (Proverbs 3:13-17)

That's quite a dream for our children.

God has that dream for each of His little children in Appalachia. Through our child development centers we are opening the eyes of parents to this dream, and showing children the joy of the wisdom that comes from education.

We have come a long way since those early days when we pioneered the idea of preschool for the children of poverty. We still have a long way to go before we can truly say that every Appalachian child has the opportunity to reach their full God-given potential and face a future bright with promise.

My dream now is that we can open more child development centers in the near future. We can't yet reach all the children who need our help.

As Kentucky now has mandatory programs for four, and even some three-year-olds, I hope we can take on a new challenge and expand our programs for infants and young children. Far too often we see children who barely speak at age two because they received little or no stimulation as infants. Sometimes these kids catch up—sometimes they don't. We need to teach Appalachia's mothers about the educational needs of their infants from the very first weeks of life.

I think we have two strong forces in our favor, the love of supporters all over the country who recognize that the long-term battle against poverty here in these mountains must begin with the children, and the dreams we have awakened in parents.

These dreams break down despair. When you can't see any future for yourself, you tend to just go along. When you can't see any future for your children . . . you just give up.

When you can see a future for your children, when there is hope that they can reach their full God-given potential and face a future bright with promise, it is amazing the energy and determination you can find in your heart.

In fostering those dreams for Appalachia's parents, we awaken a whole new force for change and growth: the incredible power of parents who have dreams for their children.

A Shepherd for the Sheep

. . . where children are guided through the difficult years of adolescence, and find proof that the future is worth working for . . .

Anyone who can seriously tell a teen-ager "These are the best years of your life!" has forgotten how difficult it is to grow up. They have forgotten the struggle to know yourself, the daily battle between wanting to be popular and doing what you know to be right. They have forgotten the loneliness that comes from a growing separation between a young adult and his or her parents. They can't remember the pain of feeling different from every other human being on earth, or the fear and confusion about the future that is part of every child's hurtling path to adulthood.

Among Appalachia's poorest youngsters, the path to adulthood is strewn with even more than the usual number of boulders and roadblocks. Poverty puts extraordinary stress on parents, and makes them less able to find the time or the strength to guide their children. Many Appalachian parents are themselves illiterate and little able to help their children in the critical goal of obtaining an education.

Worst of all, poverty steals the future, the beacon that normally guides young people. Ask most young people about the future and they'll say, "I can't wait until I can finish high school and get a job," or "I want to go to college," or "I can't wait to raise a family."

But what do you look forward to when there aren't any jobs, and there's no money to go to college, and starting a family without the means to support it is a nightmare?

How can there be any joy in growing up when the life of adults is so dark and depressing?

When I first came to Appalachia I was pained by the the lives of the young. It was clear to me that like youngsters everywhere, they wanted to be good. They wanted to be appreciated. They wanted to be loved. These needs were so great that, in the absence of constructive ways to satisfy them, too many children found destructive ways.

Too often they satisfied their need for love by turning to sex, and the result was often an unwed teen-age mother, and a boy without the maturity or means to support her and their child. They satisfied their need for excitement with violence, crime, or vandalism, and the result was often a young man who spent his formative years in a juvenile detention center or prison.

The plight of these children reminded me of a passage in the gospel of Matthew, "At the sight of the crowds, his (Jesus') heart was moved with pity for them because they were troubled and abandoned, like sheep without a shepherd.'' (Matthew 9:36)

Ever since I first began to meet the young people of Appalachia, I have dreamed that CAP could be a shepherd to help guide the young through the most difficult time of life.

Some years ago we began to make this dream come true by opening Teen Centers and Youth Centers. We figured that if we created attractive places for kids to come after school, we could get to know them and find out what their concerns were. We could guide them and help them get through the agony of growing up poor in a wealthy society. We could keep their hope from dying.

To attract the kids we put in ping-pong tables and pool tables. We organized activities and parties and dances. We took the kids on interesting trips and outings. I didn't care what drew them to us, as long as they came.

Once we were friends, we tried to help. We listened when a teen-ager said she wanted to drop out of school because the other kids laughed at her clothes—and then we gave her clothes from our Attic Stores. We worked with the student who couldn't get the hang of algebra, and whose parents were illiterate. We offered a shoulder to cry on when no one else remembered the pain of growing up.

We told the children about the good news of
Christ's love for each and every one of us.

We now have four Youth and Teen Centers for
youth ages 7-18. For the 948 young people who
take part in these programs, CAP is a shepherd,
guiding them towards adulthood, and hopefully
towards a new future for Appalachia.

*****

Nowhere to Go

Daryl stood awkwardly by himself at the dance.
It could have been the normal insecurity of a shy
16-year-old, or maybe Daryl was ashamed of his
dirty, torn clothes and sneakers held together with
masking tape, but Jerry, one of our teen counselors, thought there was something more.

At first Daryl hemmed and hawed and insisted
that nothing was wrong. Jerry talked with him
about other things — sports, school, home. When
they got around to "home," Daryl stopped talking.

"Is there something wrong at home?" Jerry
asked him. There was a long silence . . .

"I don't have a home. I'm sleeping in the alley
out back tonight."

When Jerry pressed for an explanation, the truth
came rushing out. Daryl's father died some years
ago. Daryl knew his mother didn't have any money
and that life was hard for her, but he said she didn't

understand him. They argued constantly.

"She told me to get out and never come back!"

Jerry talked with Daryl for several hours before they went to see his mother. It was late at night, and the conversation with Daryl's mother was strained, but with Jerry's help as an objective referee, Daryl and his mother came to understand how much they needed each other.

Daryl has moved back home and we've helped out by providing clothes and a winter jacket. We're keeping a close eye on Daryl these days, helping him learn to live with his mother and do what he can to help her through her struggles.

I thank God Jerry had the insight to talk to Daryl that night at the dance. Without his intervention at that point, Daryl would probably be homeless, and he almost certainly would have dropped out of school.

Keeping teens in school is one of our biggest dreams. This area has one of the lowest high school graduation rates in the country. In America's modern economy where most good paying jobs require not only a high school diploma but a college degree, a young person who drops out of school is terribly handicapped.

I'm proud of our success, not only in helping children stay in school, but also in convincing kids who have already dropped out to give it another try. Like the good shepherd, we try to keep the flock in the fold, and we make every effort to gather in those who stray.

The Blind Leading the Blind

When Don said he wanted to do an electrical project for the upcoming 4-H fair, Kevin was hesitant. Kevin had organized a 4-H club for the local kids, and encouraged them to enter projects in the fair, but he didn't know anything about electricity. It would be a case of the blind leading the blind.

Don, like many Appalachian kids, had a lot of native intelligence, but very little self-esteem. He insisted that he was dumb, and couldn't do anything right. Kevin wanted to help build up Don's confidence, and this project seemed like a great way to do that. All Kevin had to do was conquer his own lack of confidence.

For hours they worked on the electrical circuit Don had picked out, but hard as they tried they couldn't get it to work. Finally, they gave up for the day, and Don took the equipment home to continue trying to get it to work.

"I'll keep trying," Don said, "but I doubt it will work. I'm not smart enough for this."

When Don left, Kevin was discouraged too. He feared he had led Don in over his head. He was afraid this experience was just going to be one more failure to knock Don's confidence even lower.

He was pleasantly surprised, however, when he got a jubilant call from Don several hours later.

"I got it to work! I got it to work!"

Poverty destroys self-esteem, and Appalachia's children have too few opportunities to be proud of their efforts. Through our programs for teens and youngsters we try to build kids up.

One way to build children up is to get them involved in community projects. Our kids may not have money, but they have energy and talent. They can clean up trash along the roads, or paint an elderly woman's house, or plant flowers in the town center. It's great to watch them find the love and acceptance they so desperately need by building and creating beauty, instead of tearing down and destroying. Generosity and charity are tremendous esteem builders.

*****

Our Youth and Teen Centers are a wonderful step towards guiding youngsters through the difficult years of adolescence, and proving to them that the future is worth working for. But we need to do much more. My dream now is to open several more Teen Centers in the next few years, and provide more scholarships for young people who want to go to college but can't afford it.

We've also got to continue to build the economy of Appalachia so our youngsters can dream about the future with a reasonable chance for those dreams to come true. I believe in the youth of Appalachia. They are bright and eager to show their goodness. I have seen what they can do . . . all they need is a good shepherd and a dream.

A Dream Of Literacy

. . . where the love of learning takes root in all generations and people continue to grow throughout their lives . . .

In Chapter One I said it was easier to move the foothills than the mountains. That's why our first dream for education in Appalachia began with children. Once that mustard seed of a dream had been planted, however, our attention turned to the mountains—the adults. Jesus said we could move mountains, so we decided to test our faith and our vision and see if we could make a new dream work.

The counties of Appalachia are one of the least educated areas of America. In much of the rest of America, industry is based on technology, and education is critically important. For most of this century, industry in Appalachia has been based primarily on coal—where strong backs, not necessarily strong heads, are required.

When kids dropped out of school, no one made a big deal out of it. The mines didn't require a high school diploma. No one made much of an effort to convince children to stay in school, or to recapture those who dropped out. Often kids who really hadn't learned anything were passed from grade to grade. It was easier to keep them moving along than it was to convince them that they needed to learn.

That lack of concern for education still haunts us today. With money so tight all the time, many young people still drop out to go to work. Unfortunately, the job they find, if they find one, is usually part-time and at minimum wage. It's not long before they realize you can't support a family on that kind of work.

The first part of our dream was to help adults who had dropped out of high school. We wanted to help them study for a High School Equivalency Certificate (often called a General Equivalence Diploma, or G.E.D.). We began by holding classes wherever we could find space. Again, this dream took strength from those that came before. We often used our child development centers and other CAP buildings for G.E.D. classes. We encouraged people who frequented our Attic Stores and parents whose children were in our child development centers to come to these classes.

For some people it only took a few months, for others it took years, but to see the pride on their faces when they passed the test and received their G.E.D. was uplifting. With new confidence and the new credentials of a high school diploma, many went on to better jobs, or even to college.

God was clearly behind this dream and our faith in Him helped it to come true.

In our work with adults, however, we continued to find people who needed far more than a little tutoring. They couldn't read a newspaper, a book, the Bible, or anything beyond street signs. They were functionally, and in many cases, completely illiterate.

Our dream of educating adults grew even more bold. What if we could teach illiterate adults to read? Some of them might make it all the way to a G.E.D. and that would be a tremendous blessing. Others might not make it that far, but at least the world of books, including God's Word, would be open to them at last.

The problem was to find those people and develop a way to teach them to read that allowed them to keep their pride and dignity. Many of them refused to come to a class for fear that they would be embarrassed by their ignorance.

To get around this roadblock we brought the school to them. We created a program called School on Wheels and trained tutors who could go out and hold community classes or even visit individually with adults in their homes to teach them to read, or work towards their G.E.D.

Again, the fact that CAP was a trusted friend made this possible. Many adults simply wouldn't admit that they couldn't read if they didn't trust us to let them keep their dignity.

It takes a lot of courage for a 40-year-old man to ask an 18-year-old volunteer to teach him to read.

The real dream behind these efforts was not simply to give people a certificate that said, "You are educated!" It was to change attitudes about education. When we have educated enough adults and children, the process will begin to take on a life of its own. When parents begin to see what a G.E.D. means to their own life, they are less likely to allow a child to quit high school. When an illiterate adult sees what education has done for a close friend, he or she will want that same knowledge, opportunity and pleasure that comes from knowing how to read.

The dream that led to these programs is a much needed one here in these mountains. Even today, when everyone around the world is talking about education, only about two thirds of our students finish high school and some even drop out before finishing grade school.

*****

For His Kids

Nick is 33 years old and he can't read. He's not stupid and there isn't a lazy bone in his body, but he just never learned to read. He was raised on a farm in a family of 12 children. Farming in these steep, rocky hills has never been easy, and Nick's father needed his help to grow food to feed the family. Consequently, Nick rapidly fell behind in school and by the third grade he was hopelessly lost. Not long after that he stopped going to school at all.

Today he works one job at a sawmill and another job at a farm to try and support his family. He swears, "I don't want my kids to have to work as hard as I do to survive."

Nick's plan for his children begins with himself. He has decided that he wants to learn to read so that he can help his three-year-old daughter. Tears well up in his eyes when he talks about how he wants her to go to college someday—and how ashamed he is that he couldn't even read her a children's book.

A CAP employee named Lisa has been working with Nick. He gets down on himself sometimes. Years of hiding his illiteracy and feeling inadequate around others has convinced him that he isn't very smart. But he is determined, and he's making progress. He is now able to read a story to his little girl and he is starting to read newspapers.

His goal is to stay ahead of his little girl. My prayers go out to him and I wish him all the best.

I Want To Rely On Myself

"Someday, I'll be able to support my children

without having to rely on anyone else. That's what I'm living for.''

Betty has not had good luck relying on others. She married young, believing that her husband would support her. Now, at age 23, after two failed marriages and three children, she has decided to take matters into her own hands.

Betty dropped out of school in the tenth grade and never went back. She is an extremely bright woman, however, and with just a little tutoring and encouragement, she received her G.E.D. just three months after starting on it.

That's not enough for Betty. She knows she'll need more if she wants to find a good job in today's economy. Betty is now studying to become a nurse. With her determination and intelligence, I'm sure it won't be long before she reaches that goal as well.

Betty has also become an advocate of education in her community. She is making sure her children get a good education, and she tells other women whose circumstances are similar to hers (there are far too many in Appalachia) that they, too, should get an education.

*****

Earlier I mentioned that we tried to awaken the dreams of parents for their children through our child development centers. Through our G.E.D. programs and School on Wheels, our dream has been to get parents to dream for themselves as well.

We want them to realize that their lives are not over. They don't have to accept poverty and ignorance. They can still have a future.

We also want to bring the pure aesthetic beauty of learning to Appalachia. Jesus said, "The truth will set you free." I believe that's true. Reading and education bring the whole world as close as the local library. They remove the physical boundaries of geography and distance that separate Appalachia from the rest of America.

Because of CAP's work in educating adults, the dream is gaining momentum. Every adult who gets his or her G.E.D. is an inspiration to children. Every man or woman who has the courage to say, "I can't read," and the determination to learn, is an inspiration to others in similar straits. Learning is taking root across the generations and people are discovering the joy of continuing to grow in knowledge and wisdom throughout their lives.

We need to do much more and we have to be creative about it. A short time ago we purchased an old school bus. We took out the bus seats and put in classroom seats. We painted the outside red and decorated it like a "little old schoolhouse," but it's the only "little old schoolhouse" I know of that has a computer! We drive the bus out to the hollers, park it and say "school's in session!" When the class is over, we move on.

The mobile school is just one more way that we can be family, and friends, and bring something good and beautiful to the poor in Appalachia — just one more way to make the dream of literacy come true in the hollers.

A Family for Appalachia

*. . . where there is no loneliness and no begging,
only family members working together to triumph
over the bad times . . .*

I grew up in a family of 11 children, surrounded
by loving adults including my parents, uncles,
aunts, grandparents and all. Though my formative
years were passed in the very depths of the Depression and my family was poor, I can't recall a crisis
when we ever felt alone, or unable to cope. The
reason was family.

When one family member was in trouble, the
others pitched in. There wasn't any begging. You
hardly had to even ask for a hand, usually it was
offered before you asked. No one felt beholden
to anyone else because you repaid your debts by
helping the next family member who needed help.

My family wasn't perfect, but we overcame our
difficulties together. I've always felt that God has
always meant for us to live as one big family.

When CAP first began to grow, I dreamed we
could become that kind of family. In the early '50s,
the coal boom brought on by World War II ended,
and tens of thousands were laid off all over

Appalachia. Many gave up and moved away. We lost as much as a third of the families in some counties.

Even after so many moved out, there still weren't enough jobs for those who remained. Crushing poverty roared back into Appalachia close on the heels of those last coal trains of the war.

Seeing people beg was one of the things that hurt me most when I first began to serve the poor in Appalachia. Begging is against the nature of Appalachia's people. Their ancestors needed no one. They carved a life out of the mountains, separated from the rest of the world. I don't think people anywhere like to beg, but it rankles the people of Appalachia more than most.

I could see how much those who came to me hated to beg, but when your children are hungry and you don't have fuel to heat your house in the winter, and there isn't a job to be had, what else can you do? The saddest thing is that even when you get the food you need or the money to pay a doctor for your children, it still hurts. Begging makes you feel worthless.

My dream was to put an end to begging. I wanted the Christian Appalachian Project to create a sense of family love and responsibility to replace the begging. I wanted to offer a hand before it was asked for. I wanted to give people a way to pay back the help they needed when times were bad.

I wanted to preserve the dignity of those we helped.

The only way this dream could work was if we truly got to know the people. We wanted to spread a web of love through the community so we'd know when someone was in need. Out of this dream came CAP's Outreach Program.

We sent CAP volunteers and workers out to meet the people most likely to be in need. We visited the elderly, and families with young children. Most of our visits were strictly social and often that was what people needed most of all, just to know that someone, somewhere, cared whether they lived or died. When we'd gained people's confidence and trust, we learned about their troubles and needs.

An elderly woman was afraid to walk to her outhouse in the winter because of the ice. A single mother with two children didn't have enough food. A young father needed help to buy eyeglasses for his daughter.

We did what we could to fill the needs we saw. We built an indoor bathroom for the elderly woman. We helped the young mother plant a garden. We loaned the father money to buy glasses.

Whenever possible, we asked that those we helped pay us back by volunteering in a CAP program. Sometimes this meant working in one of our Attic Stores. Other times it meant helping us repair someone else's home. In some way or another we found a way for them to pay back the debt and keep their pride and dignity.

Today the Outreach Program is, in many ways, the trunk from which most of CAP's other programs branch. By helping during crisis, we meet children who could benefit from our child development center. We learn the names of elderly people who are lonely and isolated and could benefit from our elderly visitation program. We see whose house is falling down and might need aid from our Home Repair Program. We know when a family is going hungry and could use seeds and help from our Garden Seed Program.

Accepted and treated as family throughout Appalachia, we help thousands to get the aid they need without suffering the shame of begging.

*****

The Way Out Or The Way Down?

I find it hard to even imagine the panic a woman must feel when her husband is sentenced to prison and she is left to care for three children on her own, the youngest still a toddler. Tony and Barbara never had much, but they had always managed to scrape by until Tony lost his job and then was arrested for burglary.

I can't condone what Tony did. The Bible tells

us very clearly, "Thou Shalt Not Steal." But when I open my heart, I can understand the desperation that drove him to crime.

When Barbara came to see us, Tony had just been sentenced to two years in prison. Barbara had no money, her husband was in prison, she had no food, and the water had just been turned off because the bill was overdue.

It breaks my heart to see a family spiral down when poverty deals them too many blows at once. Tony reached out in desperation for what he thought was a way out, only to find it was really a way farther down.

One of CAP's most important functions is to step in before this happens. I wish Tony had come to us first.

We helped Barbara pay the water bill and she paid us back by working in one of our warehouses. Our Garden Seed Program gave her seeds and helped her to plant a full garden.

The Garden Seed Program is one of my favorite CAP programs. Rather than continually supply a family with food, we hand them seeds and say, "Here, take this plot of land, plant these seeds, fertilize them, hoe them, in due season God will send an increase, and you can pick the fruits of your own labor."

It's degrading to have someone give you food as if you were a street beggar . . . but it's uplifting to turn your own efforts into a rich harvest.

The steady growth of a garden makes you feel there's hope. The world hasn't ended. The cycles of the seasons continue. God hasn't really abandoned us.

We don't just give vegetable seeds, we also distribute flower seeds. This may seem frivolous, but "man does not live on bread alone, but on every word that comes from the mouth of God." The flowers and other beautiful things of this earth are part of God's Creation—His Word—and I believe God meant for us to enjoy them. He knows we need more than just bread.

It's wonderful to see a family transform what was once a barren, washed out yard into a bountiful garden surrounded by flowers.

With the seeds we gave her, Barbara immediately set to work planting a garden. We also helped her make home repairs that she couldn't do without Tony's help. We enrolled her children in Camp Andrew Jackson, one of our summer camps, and gave Barbara the emotional support she needed to be brave and strong.

Tony is studying for his High School Equivalency Certificate while in prison. He wants more than ever to support his family. His behavior in prison has been so good that he will probably be released early.

Tony and Barbara have a long way to go before they are reunited and back on their feet, but I think they are going to make it. I am honored that in their time of need they turned to God through us.

Helping the Helpers

Lester never needed CAP's help. In fact, Lester is famous up and down the ridge where he lives for his own generosity to those in need. He was always driving someone to a doctor's appointment, or helping someone paint a house or plant a garden. He was never too busy for a friend, and he never asked for anything in return.

A few months ago Lester collapsed suddenly and was rushed to the hospital where doctors discovered he had had a major stroke. They operated on him to remove a cerebral aneurysm, but Lester slipped into a coma from which he has not recovered.

For once, the man who helped everyone needed help himself.

After staying with him around the clock for three months, his family has brought Lester home to care for him there. We have tried to do as much as possible to help his family make it through this difficult time. We've helped them pay some of the enormous bills that are piling up, and have provided some of the medical supplies they need to care for Lester at home. We continue to pray that someday soon Lester will come out of his coma and recover.

People like Lester hold a special place in my

heart. The people around the country who send gifts to support CAP's work, even though they've never met me, or the people we help, are likewise dear to me. One of my dreams is that we can do something for them . . . that we can make them feel a part of our big family here in Appalachia.

One thing we certainly can do for our friends around the country is pray for you as we pray for Lester. If you ever have a need, please let me know. We have prayer sessions every morning at CAP, and every Friday we pray for the special requests of our friends.

*****

When I founded CAP more than 25 years ago, I dreamed of a big family, where there is no loneliness and no begging, just good people working together to triumph over the bad times. Today, CAP is that family and we have come a long way. The family still isn't big enough, however. We need more volunteers. We need more supporters. We need to help more Appalachian families and welcome them into this loving family.

We especially need your prayers. Just last week I received a call from a man in Washington, D.C. His mother had followed and supported CAP's work in Appalachia. Though she is now in her 60s, she dreamed that she could come to the hills as a CAP volunteer to help the poor.

Then cancer struck. She is now bed-ridden and

unable to care for herself, never mind volunteer. In fact, her doctors give her only a few weeks to live. Her son wanted to know if I could call her and give her comfort. I talked to her and let her know we were praying for her. I told her I would offer up my daily Mass and my own suffering for her. I asked her to pray for us and give her suffering to God for our work. This would make her a volunteer in a very special way.

Sobbing with tears, she assured me she would. When I got off the phone I, too, started to cry.

The goodness of the people in this world is amazing, and the reach of CAP's family astounds me.

Recently a man I had just met asked me if the Christian Appalachian Project was a charity. I said no—it is an act of love. I guess distances mean nothing when love is strong.

I still dream about how much an even bigger CAP family could do to help to erase poverty and bring God's love to His people in Appalachia.

Dreams of Home

. . . where every family, and every senior citizen can enjoy the warmth and safety of a good home . . .

When I first came to the mountains in 1950, I was given a church on Chestnut Street in Berea, KY. Actually, it wasn't really a church, it was a house I was to use as my home and my church. As I looked over the house with the eyes of my father, my grandfather, and my great grandfather, all of whom had been carpenters, it wasn't hard to see that the structure needed a lot of work.

The porch had collapsed, and the posts that held up the porch roof were rotted. The floors inside sagged terribly. When I went down into the basement, I saw that a previous owner had dug a hole and installed a furnace. They must have miscalculated the size of the furnace, however, because in order to make it fit, they had cut out a section of the main beam that should have been supporting the floors above.

In those, my younger, days I wasn't afraid to tackle a big job like that, so with the help of my brothers and my father, I soon had the porch repaired and the house propped up.

I've always been very proud of the craft my father passed on to me. There is a certain pride that comes from building something good and lasting like a home, a school, or a church, that is impossible to get any other way.

Most of my brothers went into various construction and carpentry trades, and I guess in a way I, too, am still in the business of building. Most of my work has been to build communities of faith, and to construct the Christian Appalachian Project. Once in a while, though, I still like to get a real hammer in my hand.

By the time my own home and church was repaired, I had already begun to meet some of Appalachia's poorest people. When I visited them at their homes, I was often shocked. Many people lived in structures for which the name "shack" would be a compliment. Many were without running water or electricity. I was amazed at how many people were still using outhouses.

There were a great many people who lived in small mobile home trailers perched precariously on the sides of the hills. Often the trailers were rusting away and threatening to fall into a creek.

The homes I saw often had holes in the floors and walls, little insulation to keep out the cold mountain winters, and windows boarded up or covered with cardboard. The more I looked, the worse things looked. Many homes were heated with wood or coal stoves that weren't properly installed for safety. Those homes that were wired for electricity often had old, unsafe wiring. I was amazed at how busy the local fire department was trying to put out the fires that resulted.

I guess it was my background, and my desire to get a hammer in my hand once in a while that gave me the idea for a new dream. I dreamed that by helping people repair and improve their homes, we could make life a little easier and a lot safer for Appalachia's poorest people.

When you live in a shack, you feel like someone who lives in a shack. You begin to accept poverty and feel you aren't worth anything. You think, "Those people with the nice, snug houses must be better than I am."

My dream was that we could, little by little, erase those feelings and help people take pride in their homes. I felt certain that this would bring new hope to the hills and hollers.

In the beginning of what has now become CAP's Home Repair Project, most of the work was done by my brothers and other friends from my home town back in Northern Kentucky. They'd all pile in a truck and come down with their tools and some building supplies, and we'd do whatever we could to keep an elderly woman's house from falling down, or put a new roof on a young family's trailer.

It wasn't long before I realized that this wasn't

nearly enough. In order for my dream to come true, this work had to go on day after day, year after year. There was a long way to go.

We began to recruit volunteers from all over the country, who came for a few weeks, or a month, or even all year round. We found out about people's needs through our other programs, especially our Outreach Program, and we did the best we could to meet those needs and provide a safe, warm home.

The program immediately had a ripple effect. One elderly woman whose home was now livable took in an old friend who had nowhere else to live. By helping one woman, we helped two women find comfort in each other's company, and in their safe home. After we provided materials and helped repair the home of a young family man, he helped out on projects for other families, helping to make our limited resources go further.

As in all our programs, we ask those we help to return the favor in whatever way they can.

Today, the Home Repair Project works around the seasons, and last year we made dreams of comfort and safety come true for more than 860 families in ten counties.

*****

A Home for the Whole Neighborhood

Melanie and Roger's house is only just barely their own. At any time there are likely to be a handful of neighbors on the front porch, and a half a dozen chatting in the small living room. One reason their house has become the center of the community is that Melanie and Roger are so friendly and generous. Another is that theirs is about the only house in the holler with running water and a shower.

When we found out that the house was in desperate need of siding and new windows, we wanted to help. Melanie and Roger didn't have the money to make the repairs. In addition to rewarding Melanie and Roger's generosity, we figured that keeping their house in shape would benefit the whole neighborhood.

With help from the neighbors, our home repair crew had the house redone with inexpensive but serviceable siding in no time.

Our hope is that this project will give others in the neighborhood the inspiration to improve and take pride in their own homes. We'll be there to help if they need us. Maybe someday, Melanie and Roger can have their bathroom back, although I suspect their front porch and their living room will always be full of friends.

Making Three Rooms Out of Two

The building that Carrie and her two children live in barely justifies the word house. It has three rooms, one a living room so small that it is dominated by the wood stove that is the building's only source of heat. One of the other rooms had so many holes in the walls that it was unusable. Carrie and her two little girls lived in just two rooms, without even a kitchen.

During the week of last Thanksgiving, six CAP volunteers from Loras College in Iowa made the trip to Carrie's house and made the third room of the house usable by replacing the rotting floor, and insulating and finishing the walls. With a few materials and a lot of sweat, they turned Carrie's two room house into a three room house.

Carrie is thrilled to have space to set up a kitchen. She still doesn't have running water, and, although the house is wired for electricity, she can't afford to pay the bill.

I hope in the near future we can find some other volunteers to help Carrie add a bathroom and running water.

In our Home Repair projects we try, as much as possible, to repair whatever structure exists. Often it just isn't worth it. Carrie's home was right on that edge. When we decide that a home isn't worth saving, and the need is very great, we sometimes will build a new house from scratch. We have a few designs that we've found to be quick and easy and inexpensive to build. These aren't fancy homes, but at least they are dry and warm.

I can't say enough about volunteers like those

college kids from Iowa. Rather than go home for Thanksgiving break to watch football games and relax from their studies, they chose to come and repair the home of a young woman struggling to raise two little girls in Appalachia.

I hope the satisfaction they gained from doing something worthwhile for a sister in need will reward them for their sacrifice.

*****

We still have a long way to go before every family and every senior citizen can enjoy the warmth and safety of a good home. There are still far too many families living in shacks. There are too many people, especially the elderly, living in homes that are fire hazards, or unsafe for other reasons.

To keep alive the dream that has become our Home Repair Project, I always look to the Christmas story for inspiration. I think about the Holy Family and their search for a place to lay their heads on that cold night. Jesus was born in an old drafty stable. He deserved more.

We can't do anything about that night nearly 2,000 years ago, but we can help those in Appalachia who live in shacks not much different from that stable in Bethlehem. We can reach out to Jesus by reaching out to our neighbors in Appalachia. We can bring warmth and safety to the Christ Child by bringing warmth and safety to the poor. They, too, deserve more.

Lorraine Corsale

Education can make her dreams come true...

Appalachia needs more child development programs geared toward building healthy minds and bodies for poor children.

Father Beiting looks on as pre-schoolers at a child development center enjoy a nutritious snack -- something many of their families can't afford to give them. Jeff Rogers

A CAP worker helps a handicapped toddler take his first steps. Exercise and therapy are critical in helping children with disabilities through their formative years.

Lorraine Corsale

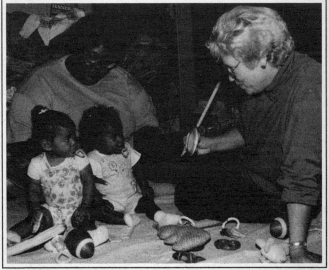

Appalachian families don't want handouts -- they are a proud people. What they want is the opportunity to help themselves.

No job is too strenuous if you have someone to share the burden with you.

There is a great need in Appalachia for more educational, recreational and independent living programs for young adults -- including the handicapped.

Father Beiting pays visit to senior citizen. Isolation and loneliness are common problems for the elderly poor in Appalachia.

Lorraine Corsale

Jeff Rogers

Shown here with Mike McLaughlin, CAP's president, Father Beiting not only loves Appalachia's people, but its hills and hollers as well. He has been serving the poor in this area for more than 40 years.

A Dream for the Autumn Years

. . . where the elderly are remembered, honored for their wisdom, and allowed to live with dignity . . .

When I was a young man first starting out in this work, I identified most with Appalachia's young people. Now, having passed my 68th birthday, I suppose it's only natural that my thoughts turn more and more to the elderly. Once upon a time, I sympathized with their aches and pains and occasional feelings of helplessness—now I truly understand.

I was taught to respect the wisdom of age. God said, "Honor your father and your mother, that you may have a long life" (Exodus 20:12). My grandparents and great-grandparents held a place of honor in our home. Even when infirmity weakened the elders, they were not forgotten. I was taught to care for them, as they once cared for me. I was taught to visit frequently to make sure that the pain of loneliness wasn't added to the already heavy burdens of illness.

Softened by that kind of training, my heart went out to the seniors of Appalachia. I found so many old people, especially women, living in run-down cabins, chicken coops, even old school buses. The conditions they lived under would have been difficult for the young and strong. For the old they were torture. Many lived in drafty shacks with no heat. Those who had heat usually used a wood or coal stove, which meant they had to haul the fuel to warm their house—no easy task when arthritis or other infirmities slowed them down. Often they lived without indoor plumbing and used an outhouse, even in winter. I met so many who were nothing but skin and bones because they had no food in the house.

Worst of their trials was the loneliness. The saddest elders were those who were isolated and had no family. Weeks would sometimes go by before they'd see another human being. Solitary confinement is considered the worst punishment for criminals. Many of Appalachia's elderly live that punishment year after year.

Others had family, but the families had fled Appalachia and now lived far away. Some might say, "Well if the elderly are so lonely and isolated, why don't they move to where there are more people?" I don't think that's fair. Even if Appalachia's elderly had the money to move, it's hard to face that kind of change when you are old. The home you live in holds tender memories, even if it is just a shack. That's the room your little boy slept in so long ago. There's the porch your husband built before he died. There's the apple tree your mother planted seventy years ago. As bad as it may look, this is your home.

My dream in those early days, a dream that grows more urgent each year as my personal understanding of the plight of Appalachia's elderly grows more real, was that we could be a friend to the seniors of Appalachia. We could be the honoring family they so greatly needed.

We began by simply visiting. Sometimes all an old woman needs to make her days more livable is someone to talk to once in a while. An old man might need someone to drive him to his doctor's appointment, or help him haul wood from his shed. An elderly couple might need seeds, canning jars and a little help to harvest and preserve food to supplement their meager food budget.

Of all those CAP helps, the elderly appreciate our friendship most. Many seniors tell me they count down the hours between our visits.

A little more than ten years ago we developed a new dream. We were concerned about seniors who had no home at all, or who simply couldn't live alone anymore. Our dream was to create a senior citizen home where the elderly could live as privately and independently as possible.

That dream came true when we purchased a small motel. The motel already had private rooms and bathrooms. To turn it into the Emmaus Christian Life Center, all we had to do was add a kitchen, a communal dining room and a living room.

At the Emmaus Center our seniors live with dignity and privacy, while sharing each other's company. This eases the aching loneliness, while providing a comfortable, safe home. Rent is set by each resident's ability to pay.

One of the most satisfying achievements of CAP is to see our dream for the elderly begin to come true. Over the years we have built up a tremendous amount of trust and confidence among the elderly of Appalachia. Many of those who are now older can remember CAP's early years, and "that young Catholic preacher." It gives me great joy to see them turn to us now because they know we will help them as friends, and honor them with the dignity they deserve.

*****

Wood, Coal and Water

Only too well do I understand Virgie's frustration with being old. Virgie is 75 years old and until recently she never needed anyone's help. She and her old wheelbarrow made a great team for bringing wood and coal in from the shed. A lifetime of walking in the mountains gave her strong legs, so she never much minded the half mile walk downhill to get drinking water, and the half mile walk back uphill to her home.

For a while after arthritis began to slow her down, she ignored the pain and continued to fend for herself. But little by little, Virgie's simple chores were becoming an ordeal.

One of the things that I find most admirable about Appalachia's elderly is their determination and ability to work hard, even into old age. Many of them grew up before electricity, automobiles and other labor-saving devices came to the mountains. A lifetime of hard work has made them tough as nails.

Even nails can rust and bend, however, and the ravages of time slow us all. Some would say, "If Virgie can't care for herself anymore, then she should be moved to a home for the elderly." I wouldn't want to try to tell Virgie that, not if she had any sort of weapon close by.

I think what CAP's volunteers do is a far better solution. Virgie likes her independence, and she only needs a little help. Wendy is young and strong. She doesn't mind visiting Virgie once or twice a week to bring in wood and coal, haul up some water from down the road, and maybe sit and chat for a while.

Someday, if she can't care for herself anymore, Virgie may indeed need to go to a nursing home, but until that time her dream is to stay in the home she cherishes. Wendy is honored to help make that dream come true.

Our 84 Year Old College Student

Emma was one of our first residents at the Emmaus Center. I don't know if she set a record, but she must have been close when she decided to go back to college at age 84.

Back in the 1920s, Emma was one of the few young people from this area to attend college, and one of the very first women. She enrolled in Berea College as a philosophy major, and was working hard on her studies when her mother died of a sudden illness. The oldest of the family, Emma felt it was her duty to help care for her younger brothers and sisters, so she quit college and went home.

Sixty years later, Emma decided to go back and finish her degree. We encouraged her dream, and after sixty years of sabbatical, she successfully applied for re-admission at Berea College, which is located just down the road from the Emmaus Center.

Emma could have picked an easier field of study, but her lifelong dream was to finish her degree in philosophy. Keeping up with her studies was difficult, especially when illness slowed her down, but if Emma had to drop a course because of poor health, she was back at it as soon as she regained her strength. Many nights you'd find her in her room, reading, writing, and studying her precious books. Her grades were high, all A's and B's, and her determination was inspiring.

Then, a few years ago, Emma found out she had advanced lung cancer. She pushed on with her studies, knowing that her time was running out.

Two years ago Emma became very ill, with excruciating pain in her hip and back. Tests showed that her cancer had spread.

Emma's dream was so close, yet it now seemed out of reach. At times she was frightened of what was to come. At other times she was a tower of bravery and strength.

At all times, she was a hero to those who knew her.

Emma died last year, just a few credits short of her dream. This is not a tale of tragedy, however, for the funny thing about dreams is that the striving alone is uplifting and inspiring. Those last five years were among the happiest years of Emma's long, full life. Everyone who met her gained something from her determination, her hope . . . her faith in her dream.

I believe there are hundreds, even thousands of Emmas among the elderly of Appalachia. If we could only give them the respect they deserve, there is so much they can offer us.

I know I'll never forget Emma's courage. The Emmaus Center will never be the same because of her presence.

*****

We've come a long way in our dream to create an Appalachia where the elderly are remembered, honored for their wisdom, and allowed to live with dignity. Unfortunately, there are still too many elderly folks living in shacks back in these hills with no one to care.

My dream now is to create several more homes like the Emmaus Center. I also wish we had more volunteers to come and visit with seniors who still live at home.

Ever since I first came to Appalachia, I have kept a tradition of preaching on street corners of isolated towns in the summer. It was an odd thing for a Catholic priest to do—Catholics don't go in for street preaching much—but I enjoyed it.

I guess my satisfaction came from the gratitude of those we met. One elderly woman told me "You brought God to us. I can't get to church no more. I miss it. I know one day I'm going to meet Jesus face to face. Church used to get me ready for that day. Your preaching and praying help me spruce up for Jesus. Thank you."

In my early years, we preached and sang to an audience made up primarily of older people. When the service was over, I'd sit and talk with them. I was amazed at how much they knew about the mountains, the people, the problems of poverty, and the reasons why programs to end poverty so often failed. I think it was then I truly began to realize that the elderly were not the burden our modern society sometimes makes them out to be. They were a source of wisdom, strength and invaluable experience that had to be cherished.

They were God's gift to young and foolish dreamers like myself.

Dreams for the Families

*. . . where families are sacred, and the home is
a place of peace, love and safety . . .*

As a young man, I held two truths about families. First was that as long as a family stuck together, they could make it through any trial. Second was that families were places of absolute safety and love.

When I came to Appalachia, both those illusions were shattered.

I suppose I was naive to believe these two truths were absolute. I had grown up in a large family surrounded by many children, two parents, grandparents, and even great grandparents. There were certainly arguments, and turmoil was not unknown, but there was never violence, and we were able to stick together through bad times.

Now, as a wiser man, I know that not every family is as blessed by God as we were. In Appalachia I have seen strains on families that are just too great for them to handle alone. Even my own family could not have withstood them.

I have also seen that sometimes a home is not a place of safety, but a place of danger and violence. Spouse and child abuse are not unique to Appalachia, but we have far more than our fair share, and less ability to cope.

Poverty puts extraordinary strains on families here in Appalachia. The constant worries about money, food and shelter wear people down until they have nothing left to give to even those they love. Men often suffer crippling blows to their self-esteem when they can't find work and support their families. Sometimes their frustration erupts as violence against their wives and children.

Appalachian women often marry too young because they are desperate to escape their own abusive families, and they see no future for themselves but to have a man support them.

Couples who start too young often find themselves with several children by the time they are 18 or 20, and without the maturity or the financial wherewithal to care for and support those children.

When I looked around in Appalachia, I was shocked to see how these forces had torn down family life over the years. We have a high percentage of out-of-wedlock births to teen-agers. We have far too much spouse and child abuse. Poverty drives too many families apart.

One of my dreams was that we could create refuges where families could be strengthened and helped through their troubles. I realized that many of our other problems stem from the breakdown of families.

When an old farm in Rockcastle County came up for sale, we decided to purchase it and turn it into a Family Life Center. We staffed the Center with marriage counselors and social workers trained to help husbands, wives and children.

The Family Life Center is sort of a crisis intervention home where families can live for a few weeks, or a few months, until they can put their lives back together and find a more permanent solution to their crisis. We help families who've been burned out of the homes, families who are in danger of divorcing, families who are homeless, or otherwise in great need. We counsel young people who are considering marriage to help them make sure they are ready.

I was also greatly concerned for women and children who were victims of domestic violence. There are few things more tragic than to see a woman whose face is disfigured by purple bruises given to her by the man she loves. We dreamed that we could provide a safe refuge for those who found the courage to escape.

That dream came true when we created a temporary refuge for abused spouses and children. At this refuge we help women realize they are not responsible for the violence of their mates. We also try to work with abusers to show them better ways to deal with frustration and low self-esteem. Our goal is to keep families together, if it is safe to do so, but our first concern is always for the safety of women and their children.

*****

Starting Over

"CAP gave me my life back!"

For 13 years Felicia lived with a man who abused her. She tried as hard as she could to meet her husband's outrageous demands, but when she failed, he would beat her terribly.

Her husband's need to control her was so great that when Felicia finally broke free and came to our spouse abuse center home with her three children, we were amazed at how helpless she was. She didn't know how to write a check, and she was uncomfortable even using a telephone.

Wife battering cuts across all socioeconomic lines, but in Appalachia a lingering tradition of absolute male domination over women makes it more common. In addition, the stress and despair of poverty drives many men to alcohol, a very common and insidious factor in spouse and child abuse. One of the things we try to teach the men who are willing to go through counseling is that they can find satisfaction in a different way. Rather than vent their anger by dominating their family, they should take pride in the role of protector and supporter. That's the role God wants parents to play.

Quite frankly, the number of men who beat their wives who can make this change in their behavior is not high. That's why we must provide refuge to people like Felicia. Felicia had left her husband before, but he always promised he'd change, so she went back. After 13 years of unending patience and forgiveness, she realized he would not, or could not, change.

Felicia stayed at our spouse abuse shelter for several weeks, so she and her children could be counseled and start down the road to emotional health. This counseling is so important. The external bruises fade fairly quickly. The internal bruises to self-esteem are much slower to heal.

Felicia and her children are on the way. After leaving our spouse abuse center, the family lived with us at the Family Life Center for three months, while Felicia slowly took control of her life again.

After being so utterly dependent on her husband for so long, Felicia is somewhat scared of this independence. Little by little, she is finding the courage to move on. Felicia has now decided to go back to school at Eastern Kentucky University to study nursing.

Thanks to CAP, and friends all over the country who support our work, Felicia and her children have a new life free from violence.

*****

Our work with families may be the most difficult we do. Our guiding light in this work is the non-judgemental love of Jesus Christ. Jesus loved everyone, the saints and the sinners. We're not here to separate and punish, we're here to help families stay together.

We're here to provide a haven for families struck by adversity. We're here to help husbands and wives strengthen their marriages. When there is abuse, we're here to comfort those in pain, and challenge those who cause pain. Most of all, we're here to make sure the children are safe and warm and loved.

We're here to make a dream come true, to make Appalachia a place where families are sacred, and the home is a place of peace, love and safety.

A Dream of Independence

. . . where the disabled are looked on not as a burden, but as a blessing—a chance to prove the worth of every one of God's children . . .

One of the hardest lessons I've had to learn over the years is that we can't help everyone. We have to focus our efforts where they are most needed. There are some who are blessed by God with brains, good mental and physical health, a strong family and good opportunities. Even when poverty surrounds them on all sides, they have a good chance to succeed without help.

But there are also people with disabilities who would need a helping hand even in the most affluent society. In the midst of poverty, their suffering is truly great. In Appalachia we have more than our share of children and adults with disabilities. It probably stems from the lack of good health care and nutrition for expectant mothers, too many births to teen-agers, and too much drug and alcohol abuse.

Whatever the reason, the more our other dreams came true, and we became family to the people of Appalachia, the more we wanted to do something to help the disabled.

At first, we tried to make their lives more joyful by simply visiting with them and taking them on recreational trips and outings. It was a start—a mustard seed of faith and dreams—but what if we could help the people with disabilities develop and make the most out of the abilities they had? What if we could help them become proud of their abilities, instead of ashamed of their disabilities? What if we could help them become more independent?

To get this dream started, we bought an old motel and turned it into a sheltered workshop for adults with disabilities. At that workshop, we once manufactured artificial corn husk flowers and other traditional Appalachian craft products like Christmas wreaths. To help support CAP's programs, we sold these fine products nationwide through catalogs and retail stores.

Working helps people with disabilities know that they are part of a solution, not part of a problem. It gives them pride to be able to earn a paycheck each week instead of always relying on others to care for them.

Today, that mustard seed of a dream for Appalachians with disabilities has grown quite a bit. Instead of directly employing a limited number of people with disabilities, CAPrice Industries now operates a Supported Employment Program that helps people with disabilities find work in local businesses. We carefully match each applicant with a job they can handle. We send a CAPrice counselor to the job site to learn the new job. The counselor then goes to work with the CAPrice worker to coach them through the first few weeks. This gives employers confidence that they'll get a well-trained worker, and helps us to convince them to give people with disabilities a chance. One of our heavy focuses is in the area of food preparation. We teach people with disabilities how to work in a large kitchen. While learning skills they can use in restaurants and motels, they provide meals for our child development centers and other CAP programs.

In addition, CAPrice teaches independent living skills to people with disabilities. These include money management skills, self-care daily living skills, and communication skills.

Through these programs we are putting the talents of people with disabilities to work, and proving their worth to society. We are helping their dreams come true.

*****

Carl the Wonder Worker

"This boy will never be able to do anything but watch T.V. and collect a disability check."

That was the assessment of one person who

knew Carl before he began working in CAPrice's Supported Employment Program. Carl was 20 years old, and had mild mental retardation. The person who held this dim view couldn't see beyond Carl's limitations. We could.

After we discussed opportunities for Carl with the managers of a manufacturing plant, they were split on whether to hire him. The general manager was willing to give Carl a try, but the production manager didn't want Carl on his team. Luckily the general manager pulled rank, and Carl was hired.

Carl's CAPrice counselor spent a few days with him on the production line, showing him how to put buttons on a strap. Carl caught on quickly, and within a few weeks he was the fastest worker in the entire plant. He had won the production manager over completely.

When another opportunity with more hours came up at a building supply store, Carl wanted to take the chance. He applied and won the job. Again, he outdid even our expectations. He has an excellent memory and can locate inventory in the store's warehouse faster than anyone else. His attitude with customers is outstanding, and his employer thinks Carl will someday make an excellent salesperson.

While his career was taking off, Carl's maturity and communication skills grew dramatically. He also learned the joy of giving, something he had never experienced before. Throughout his life, he had always been on the receiving end of things. Last year, with his own money, Carl bought his father the first Christmas gift he'd ever given anyone. He was tremendously proud.

Just how far Carl has come is evidenced by the fact that the manufacturing plant that first hired Carl wants him back. They've offered him a full-time job at full wages and benefits. Carl is now one of the most valued workers in town. Not too bad for a young man who ''will never be able to do anything but watch T.V. and collect disability.''

Carl's story is not unique. There is so much God-given talent waiting to be tapped for the good of the whole family of humanity. If we just give it a chance to shine, we'll be blessed a hundred times over. There are a lot more Carls out there waiting to blossom.

I think there is also a parallel between Carl's story and the story of Appalachia. So many people have written Appalachia off without giving her people a chance to show what they can do. Just like Carl, Appalachia's poor just need a helping hand for a while until they can stand on their own. Then you'll see the natural talents and strength of her people win the day.

Just as Carl has now become a much valued employee, Appalachia could someday be the most valued economic area in America. A dream? Maybe . . . but I think it's a dream worth a try.

*****

Some years ago I had a secretary named Marilyn who had a secret dream of her own. Marilyn had been taking courses after work, working towards a masters degree in education. When she asked me if she could take a summer off to finish her degree, I reluctantly let her go. She was a very good secretary, and I hated to lose her, but you should never hold a good dream down.

When Marilyn returned after that summer she pulled me aside. She said that now that her own personal dream to get her masters degree had come true, she had a new dream—a dream for CAP.

She was concerned about children with disabilities, especially those with severe multiple disabilities. These children are often institutionalized because meeting their needs is considered beyond the abilities of parents.

In her studies, Marilyn had learned about early intervention programs that help these children develop, and help their parents learn to care for their children at home.

Marilyn's dream was that we could start such a program for the people of Appalachia. She wanted to tell parents that they could be the best teachers and caregivers for their own children.

"Well, let's try it," I said.

Marilyn's dream was the mustard seed that became a program we call Parents-Are-Teachers. Through weekly meetings with families, we help the parents of children with special needs learn to meet the medical and developmental needs of their children.

Parents are thrilled to have the support, and overjoyed to see the difference this help makes in the lives of their children. Often our workers and the parents are able to help a child become more independent. This improves the life of the child and lessens the burden on parents.

One of the things we discovered early on is that even the most dedicated parent needs a break from the 24-hour-a-day, seven-days-a-week routine of caring for a child with special needs. A new dream was that we could find a way to give them a break—a respite from their duties.

This dream was the birth of the Rainbow Respite Care Center. This program provides short-term care at the Rainbow Respite Care Center, or at home, for children and adults with mental and physical disabilities.

Rainbow Respite gives parents and other care-givers a chance to relax. It gives them the opportunity to do things they couldn't otherwise do, such as visit with friends, go out to a movie, or just take a walk. It gives them time to recharge their parental batteries and helps them be more loving and patient when the respite is over.

I'm so glad Marilyn had the courage to come to me with her dreams. Because of her dreams, the Parents-Are-Teachers and Rainbow Respite

programs now help a great many families who
have children with special needs.

*****

Standing on His Own

Joey wanted to stand on his own. He never said
this, because he hasn't yet learned to talk, but his
desire didn't need words.

At three years old, Joey should have been walking and running, but serious physical and mental
developmental delays have slowed him down. He
would inch his way across the floor until he
reached a chair or other piece of furniture, and
pull himself up. Then he'd stand on his wobbly
legs and look out across what must have seemed
to him to be an enormous distance between the
support he was holding and the next nearest
hand-hold.

He wanted to let go, but his legs just couldn't
hold him.

Joey's parents had to carry him everywhere, no
easy task with a 30-pound toddler. But what was
far more disturbing was that Joey's progress was
stalled. He'd gone as far as he could on his own,
now he needed help.

That help came when Joey's parents enrolled
him in our Parents-Are-Teachers (PAT) program.
Gloria, his PAT caseworker, showed his parents

special activities and exercises that could assist Joey in his development, both physical and mental.

Every baby's first steps are cause for celebration, but when Joey finally let go and took his first brave steps, the cheers of his parents could be heard halfway across the county.

When we begin working with a family like Joey's, we usually focus our attention not on the child, but on the parents. Before they can be teachers we have to build up their confidence and self-esteem. So many parents blame themselves for their children's disabilities. We try to show them that God has a plan for every child, and that those with special needs invariably come with "special gifts." A child with special needs is not a burden, he or she is an opportunity for loving and giving that most parents will never enjoy.

Many parents will see their children take their first steps, but few will get as much joy and accomplishment from it as Joey's did.

One of the stumbling blocks we often face is that many Appalachian parents, because they are undereducated, or even illiterate, don't think they can handle the special therapies and treatments that could help their children. One of the benefits of the Parents-Are-Teachers program is that we prove to those parents that they can care for their children. When they succeed, their new found sense of accomplishment and confidence often carries over into the rest of their lives.

Joey is a wonderful example of what the Parents-Are-Teachers program can do. Every child wants to stand on his own as much as possible. And all parents want their children to reach the utmost of their potential. Thanks to the generosity of our supporters, the Parents-Are-Teachers program is helping them reach those goals.

Joey is now standing on his own. In fact, he's walking, running and generally causing havoc throughout the house. I don't think his mother would trade this new bedlam for all the money in the world.

Four-Eyes

Jimmy is 34 and has mental retardation. When he first began coming to Rainbow Respite, he didn't want to be with anyone. He had a hair-trigger temper, and when he was angry, he would hurl obscenities at anyone within earshot.

It took the patience of a saint to deal with him and it often wore his parents out. They were thrilled to have the chance to take a break once in a while, especially when they saw that Jimmy was making progress at the respite center that he couldn't make at home.

In the two years that Jimmy has been coming to Rainbow Respite, he has opened up quite a bit. He has made friends with several other regular visitors, and enjoys the outings and activities at the center.

He still gets angry, but the last time he lost his temper and couldn't hold his anger in, he took a long pause before he let loose with the nicest insult he could think of.

"Four-eyes!"

You wouldn't normally congratulate someone for calling another that name, but for Jimmy it was a major breakthrough.

Jimmy's parents report that he is much happier and less abusive at home these days as well. We'll continue to work with him when he visits us and who knows, maybe someday we'll get him to stop insulting people altogether. Until then, "Four-eyes!" will have to do.

*****

When Jesus and his disciples came upon a blind man one day, his disciples asked him, "Rabbi, who sinned, this man or his parents, that he was born blind?"

Jesus' answer is the inspiration for our dreams for people with disabilities in Appalachia. He said, "Neither he nor his parents sinned; it is so that the works of God might be made visible through him." (John 9:2)

CAP's programs for people with disabilities are our attempt to show the power of God's universal love. God loves the child who cannot speak or walk as much as He loves the Rhodes scholar or Olympic athlete. In that truth there is a lesson for all of us. We are all less than perfect. We all have a disability of some type or other.

In no way do our limitations make us less human, less valuable or less loved by our Father in heaven.

When we triumph over our disabilities, and when we love each other in spite of our limitations, we make the works of God visible to the world.

We have a long way to go before Appalachia is a place where people with disabilities are looked on not as a burden, but as a blessing and a chance to prove the worth of every one of God's children.

There is still a lot of God's work waiting to be made visible here in Appalachia.

A Dream of Good Health

. . . where disease no longer contributes to poverty, and the beauty of the mountains is reflected in the good health of the people . . .

One of the gifts God gives you as you get older is humility. There was a time when I thought I knew all the answers to erasing poverty from the mountains. Now that I'm wiser, I know I'm lucky if I know the right questions. And I wonder if God purposely reveals part of an answer to one person and part to another— knowing that only when we join together will dreams come true.

A few years ago, I organized a seminar on poverty in Appalachia and invited representatives from other charitable organizations, government social programs, churches and community organizations. For a full day we discussed the causes and cures of poverty in Appalachia and planned ways that we could work together to share resources and fight poverty side by side. We all learned a great deal from each other's ideas.

During our discussions, one thing stood out as a cause of poverty that had not yet been addressed: poor health.

We noted the shortage of doctors, hospitals and clinics. We talked about the lack of preventative medicine and prenatal care for women. We enumerated the health problems of Appalachia's senior citizens.

There's an old saying that "if you haven't got your health, you haven't got anything." In Appalachia, that saying should be, "if you haven't got your health, AND you haven't got anything . . . you haven't got a prayer."

The more we talked that day, the more I began to dream that CAP could play a major role in improving the health of the poor in Appalachia.

In recent years, a great deal has been learned about good nutrition, and how to prevent heart disease, diabetes, and many other illnesses that plague Appalachia. What if, rather than try to cure these diseases after they occur, we taught people how to stay healthy and avoid disease?

If we could do this, we could strike a blow at a major cause of poverty in Appalachia.

To make this dream grow, we gathered nurses, nutritionists and public health experts to study the health problems of the poor in Appalachia.

They identified bad drinking water as a major danger. Most people in Appalachia have their own wells, or use water from local streams and creeks. Unfortunately, these water sources are often contaminated by disease-causing bacteria.

Another major area where health education

could help was nutrition. Many people in Appalachia don't know the basics of good nutrition. The traditional Appalachian diet is quite laden with fat. Add to that an unhealthy balance of snack and convenience foods and it's not surprising that children often suffer from poor diets that reduce their energy and their ability to concentrate in school. If children don't eat well, they don't feel well.

Our dream to give people the information and power to protect their health has evolved into a program called the Community Health Advocates Program, CHAP for short. CHAP provides physical, mental, emotional and environmental health education to those who need it most in Appalachia.

CHAP organizes groups of local women who meet weekly to give each other support, learn about health and parenting issues, and to make crafts. CHAP talks about health, nutrition and self-esteem in our preschools, youth and teen centers, and in local schools and Senior Citizens Centers. We also visit with people in their homes to help them deal with health related issues such as diabetes, high blood pressure and prenatal care.

*****

Raisins From Grapes

In a presentation to a kindergarten class, Mary,

one of our CHAP workers, asked the children, "Where do raisins come from?"

"The store," one girl offered.

With a little more prompting, the children eventually guessed grapes. Then came the big challenge. Mary asked, "How do you get from grapes to raisins?"

One little boy rose out of his seat confidently and said, "They hatch!"

This story is cute, but the message delivered to the kids that day was very serious. One of the most pressing concerns of CHAP is to teach good nutrition to children. So many of Appalachia's poorest children live on soda and junk food. They don't eat any better because their parents don't eat any better, and bad nutritional habits are passed from generation to generation. We are trying to break that cycle.

Our Community Health Advocates are making headway. In a presentation to a group of second graders, Mary again stressed the importance of good nutrition. She even brought healthy snacks of peanut butter and crackers and juice. She was afraid, however, that her ideas were going in one ear and out the other.

She was sure that as soon as the children were out of her sight, they'd revert to soda and chocolate cake.

A few days later, Mary returned to the classroom and walked in right at snack time. She was amazed when the children proudly pointed out that they were drinking juice instead of soda.

Little by little we're helping Appalachia's children take pride in good health and nutrition. Over the long run this is going to have an enormous effect on health and the poverty that poor health often brings.

CHAP also works to build up the self-esteem of children. People who like themselves are more likely to care about their health.

At another presentation, Kathy, the CHAP presenter, asked each child to trace his or her hand, and write something good about themselves in each of the fingers. One little boy carefully traced his hand and then sat puzzled.

"What's the matter Eddie?" Kathy asked him. "Do you need some help?"

"Yeah, I just don't know what to put down."

Eddie's difficulty is all too common among the children of poor people. We have to show them, sometimes prove to them, that they are capable and worthwhile and special.

Kathy and Eddie thought together for a while until Eddie said, "I'm good at computers!"

Once he got started, Eddie filled in his hand quickly—beaming the whole while.

At the end of the session Kathy was preparing to leave when Eddie ran from across the room and almost tackled her with a little boy bear hug.

"I know why God put me in that classroom that day," Kathy remembers.

Mommy is Sick

It wasn't like Karen to miss one of CHAP's weekly women's group meetings. When she couldn't get Karen on the phone, Debbie was worried about her, so she drove out to Karen's house to see how she was doing. When Debbie knocked on the door, Karen's little girl answered.

"Mommy can't come to the door right now, she's in bed."

"Is she all right?"

"I don't think so."

Debbie entered the home and found Karen lying in bed, disoriented and uncommunicative. According to her daughter, she had been like that for several days.

After visiting with her, Debbie was convinced that Karen was suffering from clinical depression, possibly brought on by her physical health problems. Debbie went to work immediately to help Karen get the mental and physical health care resources she needed.

Debbie visits with the family every few days now, helping them find the resources they need and helping Karen deal with her illnesses.

I hate to think what might have happened to Karen and her daughter if CHAP hadn't been involved in their lives. Debbie's efforts averted a true crisis.

CHAP links families to resources that help prevent crisis and disaster. I cannot thank our supporters enough for allowing us to offer this vital service.

After adjustments to her medication, and rehabilitative therapy, Karen is now back on her feet. At the last meeting of the CHAP women's group, she was welcomed back with hugs and tears.

*****

Bringing good health to Appalachia by educating the poor to prevent illness isn't going to be easy. We need to develop new programs and we need to give them time to work, possibly a whole generation. It would probably be more immediately satisfying to just wait until people get sick and then try to help them. That, however, means a lot of suffering and lost opportunity to erase poverty. In the long run it would also be much more expensive than CHAP's approach of health care education.

It takes courage to work towards a dream when the payoff is far in the future. The workers of CHAP are like the pioneers of old in Appalachia. They are determined to break new ground to bring good health to the poor. I am immensely proud of them. They are an exciting group of people.

I know this program is going to work. Someday the dream will come true and disease will no longer contribute to poverty in the mountains. When that day finally comes, the beauty of the mountains will be reflected in the good health of the people.

Dreams to Share

. . . where our nation's abundance and generosity is put to good use to welcome the people of Appalachia back into the American family . . .

As I write this book, America is mired in a deep recession. The hot topic at many charitable organizations is the idea that because of the recession, Americans are becoming tired of the poor. They are tired of hearing about poverty.

I don't think that's true. I think Americans are the most generous people on earth. They will share even when their own needs are great—IF they believe their generosity will be well used in a program that really works.

CAP is one of those programs. That's why, while many other organizations are retreating during this recession, CAP is still moving ahead.

Even in an economic downturn, there is still enough wealth in America to lend a hand to those who are less fortunate. Tough times just mean we have to be a little more creative. I think that's a good thing.

About six years ago, we received an odd phone call from a friend that worked with the international relief agency World Vision. The Parker Brothers toy company had donated new children's books to the American Indian Heritage Foundation, and they had distributed all they could to Indian children around the country. The Foundation then asked another nonprofit organization, World Vision, if they could make use of the books, toys and games in their programs. World Vision then contacted us to see if we could distribute these items to the poor in Appalachia.

Of course, we were thrilled. We eventually received 27 tractor-trailer loads of overstocked books, toys, games and children's cassette tapes.

We distributed these toys and games to children all over Appalachia. Many went into the Christmas baskets we distribute each year to thousands of Appalachian families to help them celebrate the birth of Jesus. These baskets include food for a Christmas meal, winter hats and gloves, toys, books and other treats to bring joy on Christmas morning to families who have far too little joy in their lives.

When we had prepared our Christmas baskets, there were still trailers full of toys left over. We gave the extras to other charitable organizations and churches all over Appalachia to use in their efforts for the poor.

Those surplus toys, that might have sat in a warehouse somewhere, or been sold at a loss to a liquidator, ended up bringing joy to the underprivileged children all through the mountains.

That unique gift of toys was the first time we had ever received such a large donation of merchandise. It sparked a new dream—a dream that we could be a conduit for businesses and individuals with items they wanted to donate to the people of Appalachia.

We called this dream "Operation Sharing." We wanted to share these donations with the families we help and with other organizations helping the poor in Appalachia.

Since that gift of trailer trucks full of toys, Operation Sharing has grown by leaps and bounds, putting America's bounty and generosity to work to help the people of Appalachia.

*****

Charlie the Bull

We don't often receive gifts that are alive, or that need to be cleaned up after with a shovel, but Charlie the Bull was special. Charlie had been raised by a West Virginia teen-ager for showing at county fairs. When the young man went off to college, he and his father decided to donate Charlie to a worthwhile organization.

They called around to see who might want a 1,000 pound Charolais bull. Eventually, the offer came to us. When Charlie, the manager of Operation Sharing, got the call he immediately thought of Frank, a contact who ran a small local community organization providing services to the poor. Charlie thought of Frank because he knew Frank kept cows at home. He might know how to get some use out of this unusual gift.

"Frank, any ideas of what we can do with a Charolais bull?" Charlie asked him.

"Absolutely! We could offer him for stud. There are dozens of families around here that keep a milk cow. They have to have them bred every year to keep the milk coming and it costs between $50 and $75 to have a cow bred. We could offer the service at a much lower cost. I know some families could really use an extra fifty bucks."

Today "Charlie the Bull," no relation to "Charlie the Operation Sharing Manager," is doing his duty to help poor families in Appalachia. I don't think he minds the work. It sure beats ending up as a pile of steaks.

The story of "Charlie the Bull" is an example of how we must be creative in putting America's abundance to good use for the poor. We don't get many gifts of live animals, but we do get building supplies, food, commodities, new clothing and hundreds of other useful items. Recently, we received a million toothbrushes, which we distributed to our own health programs and health departments all over Appalachia.

A short time ago we received a truly wonderful gift of more than $200,000 worth of overstocked

Bibles and Bibles-On-Cassette from the Thomas Nelson Company, the world's largest Bible publisher. The Bibles-On-Cassette were particularly appreciated by senior citizens who can no longer see well enough to read the Good Book.

To give just a couple other examples, each year we receive trucks full of vegetable seeds from the Asgrow Seed Company to distribute in our Garden Seed Program, and to other organizations. And the Bush Brothers Cannery in Tennessee sends several truck loads of canned goods every year for inclusion in our Christmas Baskets.

Sunshine Bucks

As I mentioned earlier, we require that parents whose children attend our child development centers help out at least two days a month at the center. At one of our preschools, the Sunshine Center, we've added a special incentive for extra effort. Mothers and fathers who work beyond the required two days a month receive "Sunshine Bucks" as pay.

Twice a year we have a special sale of choice items from Operation Sharing. Parents can use their Sunshine Bucks to purchase anything from furniture to toys. Through this creative idea, we encourage parents to spend more time learning how to teach their children, we distribute useful items to the poor, and we give parents the satisfaction that comes from earning.

*****

I know there is enough wealth in America to help the poor of Appalachia, even in a recession. Through Operation Sharing we put our nation's abundance and generosity to good use to welcome the people of Appalachia back into the American family.

The gifts I mentioned here are only a few examples of what we have been able to use—or what we could use. The possibilities for this dream are limited only by our imagination.

Dreams of Our Volunteers

. . . where God's people administer His love to those in need, and those who give receive even more in return . . .

After my ordination to the priesthood, I spent a year teaching in high school. Many of the kids in my classes owed a passing grade to my generosity, so when I came to Appalachia, I kiddingly reminded them that they had a debt to repay. I suggested they could pay me back by coming to Appalachia and helping me paint buildings, fix up houses, visit with the elderly and take care of kids. Despite those passing grades, I was surprised when they said, "Okay."

I think they were even more surprised when they found they enjoyed the work a great deal.

It wasn't easy. We worked long and hard from early morning to late at night. We took on difficult tasks and never settled for the easy way out. Yet it was fun because our efforts were successful in changing the lives of the poor.

Sometimes I felt guilty because I worked those kids so hard. They had little time for recreation and they lived in crowded quarters. They had to depend on their own cooking, which was often a real cross to bear.

And yet there was a certain contagious excitement . . . a dream was being born.

Eventually, I considered my students' debt paid, and I let them off the hook. To keep the dream alive we began to recruit volunteers from all over the country. They came from all walks of life, some were still in grade school, many were college students, some were newlyweds, some were retired senior citizens. They worked a week or two or for a whole summer. Some even came for a year—and then stayed for two or three.

All were excited to be part of a dream. They felt that by putting their talents and skills to God's work, they were going to make a difference.

The truly wonderful thing was not the free labor. Even more important was the breath of fresh air, and hope, and sacrifice those volunteers brought to this tired land. The Appalachian people sensed the power of this dream and were inspired to do more to help themselves and their neighbors.

As much as our volunteers have done for Appalachia, though, I think they gain even more.

I have seen many come to us unsure about their own worth and of the direction of their lives. They leave with the well-deserved pride and sense of well-being that comes from doing God's work. They leave having held hands with the Almighty in a way you seldom do in a church.

Many of them continue to support our work even after they've gone home. They talk to a friend about their experiences, and a new volunteer is born to bless our work. Others gather people to pray for the success of our work. They talk to the old, the bedridden, and the home-bound, and ask them to remember CAP in their prayers and suffering. I can't stress enough how important that is.

Others go home and recruit local groups of children to share their toys and collect donations for the children of Appalachia. They urge government leaders to bring about change in Appalachia.

These folks' lives have been changed by volunteering with CAP.

America is full of potential volunteers. The volunteer tradition is very strong and Appalachia has benefitted tremendously from this honorable tradition. Our volunteers come, not because they feel they are better than those they help, but because they realize that we are all brothers and sisters of our Lord Jesus.

That is our dream for volunteering. We want to share as a family shares. Those who can build will build. Those who can teach will teach. Those who can pray will pray. It's the same way St. Paul encourages us to share in his letter to the Romans.

When I look back on the history of our volunteer program from those early days to the present, it amazes me to realize that nearly 40,000 people have come to volunteer with CAP. I suspect that's

more than have volunteered for any other program
of our nature in the region.

If it's true that the world's most valuable
resource is not money or raw materials but
people—and I believe it is—then our volunteers
have made a remarkable contribution of resources
to bring comfort to those who suffer in Appalachia.

*****

Fixing Up Lauri

When Lauri volunteered to lead a group of Girl
Scouts, she figured she could help them dream
about a new future for themselves. She never
counted on the girls taking such an interest in, and
dreaming about her own life.

The 10 and 11 year old girls in her troop think
Lauri is too old to be unmarried, so at every opportunity, they try to fix her up with eligible young
men. Lauri enjoys taking the girls out on field trips
because they so rarely get out of their own hollers
to see the world outside. She loves to watch shy
little girls turn into interested—and interesting—
young ladies.

The only problem is, every trip threatens to turn
into a "find Lauri a boyfriend" trip.

It's so important for young people like Lauri to
come here to Appalachia. Children like the girls
in Lauri's Girl Scout group desperately need role

models outside their own families. Too many of the adults around them, young and old, have been so beaten down by poverty that they pass their despair directly on to the young. People like Lauri break the cycle and breathe new life into Appalachia's children.

She, with her bright outlook on life and her education, has given her Girl Scouts a glimpse of what could be for them. She is proof, for one thing, that a woman can remain single past the age of 19 and not be an "old maid."

Lauri's dream is that the young girls who care so much about her will care as much about themselves as they grow. She hopes they'll dream of their own futures with hope and confidence.

Lauri is willing to do more than just hope. By giving of herself, she is helping to make her dreams for Appalachia's children come true.

The Best Friend I Ever Had

Before Paul, one of our volunteers, went to visit Susie, he was warned. People told him Susie had Alzheimer's disease, and that her speech was slurred and terribly hard to understand. Understandably, Paul approached his visit to Susie's house with trepidation.

Because of her speech problems, whatever friends Susie once had, had now given up on her and stopped visiting. She was living alone and ter-

ribly lonely in her old age, a fate that befalls many
of Appalachia's elderly.

Thank God, Paul doesn't give up easily. He
visits Susie once a week, and bit by bit he began
to understand her speech. He's not convinced that
she has Alzheimer's disease at all. She may have
suffered a stroke some time ago that makes it hard
for her to speak, but Paul says her mind is sharp.

Many people are symbolically like Susie. Hid-
den behind a speech defect or a disability or ignorance or poverty, there is a real person, a child
of God. Most people will walk away and say "I
can't understand what they are saying. It's not
worth the trouble."

Every once in a while, though, a Paul comes
along and says, "I want to get to know this person. I'll be patient, and look beyond the speech
defect, or the ignorance, or the poverty and find
the child of God. Then I will talk with my sister."

Susie loves Paul's visits, and Paul admits that
she has grown on him to the point where Susie's
front room is now the favorite stopover on his
elderly visitation rounds.

One of the most beautiful things about volunteering, especially the kind of one-on-one relationships
that we emphasize, is the feeling of being needed
and loved. Susie gets a great deal out of Paul's
visits, but Paul may get even more. At this point
in his young life, he could be wondering about the
meaning of life, and why he is on this earth. In-

stead, Paul knows, that at least at this time, he is on this earth to be Susie's only friend.

That's a mission and an occupation worthy of any saint.

A few days before Christmas last year, Paul visited Susie to bring her food and a few presents. When he knocked on the door, Susie didn't answer with her usual joy. In fact, she was crying. When Paul asked her why, she said she was feeling terribly lonely. She didn't have anyone with whom to share her Christmas. She didn't have a tree because she couldn't afford one. How could she have a Christmas without friends or family, and without a tree?

Paul stayed as long as he could, and when he left his heart was heavy. A few miles down the road he passed a sign saying, "Christmas Trees."

Ten minutes later, after rescheduling his other plans, Paul was on the way back to Susie's house with a small, but lovely Christmas tree.

When he gave it to Susie, she burst into tears again. This time they were tears of joy. When they had finished decorating the tree, Susie turned to Paul, and in a voice that only Paul, and our Father in heaven understand, she said, "You are the best friend I've ever had."

For a 75-year-old woman to say that to a young man she has only known for a year or so is remarkable. Paul will never forget that day.

One day, when Susie has long gone home to her

Father, Paul will find himself in a tough spot.
Maybe he'll be having one of those days we all
have when we feel we are unimportant and un-
loved. I know that when that happens, Susie's
words will come into his head, ''You are the best
friend I've ever had.''

That's not the kind of reward you can get from
your average job.

*****

Two years ago, I found out that a friend was
dying of cancer. He was a senator from New York
who had volunteered with CAP in his younger
years, and had brought his children down to
volunteer as well. I wanted to talk with him before
he died. For days I planned how I would thank
him for all he had done for CAP, but when I
entered his hospital room, he cut me short.

Before I could thank him, he thanked me for
giving him the opportunity to volunteer.

His surprising gratitude makes me more convinced than ever that we must expand our dream
to make Appalachia a place where God's people
voluntarily administer His love to those in need
. . . and where those who so generously give of
themselves receive even more in return.

Yes, it's true that to make our dreams come true,
we need financial support, and we are tremendously grateful for it. In addition though, we need
more people like Lauri and Paul.

I've said this enough times to bore everyone at CAP, but I still think it's true that "a happy volunteer is a tired volunteer." A tired volunteer is one who cares enough to do the very best for brothers and sisters that need help. I invite everyone in America to gain this tired, but happy satisfaction.

My brother Ray, 20 months my junior, told me a few years ago that he wanted to come to the mountains to volunteer. Like many members of my family, Ray was a carpenter. He had enlisted the support of many of his friends in the construction business, and he was sure that together they could accomplish a great deal for the people of Appalachia.

God had other plans, however.

Ray was diagnosed with Lou Gehrig's disease. At our last meeting, just before he died two years ago, he looked at me and said, "I guess I won't be helping you after all. I'm sorry. I wanted to do it so much."

I feel sure Ray is in heaven now, with that other carpenter—the one from Nazareth. I'm sure he is a great volunteer there. I imagine him recruiting others to do the job he wanted so much to do on earth. I'm sure he talks to God and says, "Lord, here's a few good prospects. Send the Holy Spirit to inspire them. Get them to Appalachia. They can do what I wanted to do."

To our volunteers in heaven I say, "Thanks and

keep up the prayers. You still touch our land with love.''

And to those whom the Holy Spirit visits here on earth, I say ''Come on! We're waiting for you here in Appalachia.''

Your Dreams

. . . where your talents and resources are put to God's work to help your brothers and sisters in Appalachia . . .

Working toward a dream is great fun. It makes each day exciting and worth living.

I hope, by writing this book, I have shown you enough of our dreams to capture your interest and convince you to join our CAP family in making these dreams come true in Appalachia.

There are many ways to take part in this dream. First, I ask you to pray for us. The power of prayer can light up a dream and raise it to the heavens. And anyone can do it.

Another way to help is to send a donation. It takes a great deal of money to run CAP's programs each month and we desperately need new supporters, so please tell your friends how much we need assistance. We also need increased help from our old supporters. If you can help, I assure you your financial support will be well used.

This year we recruited more volunteers than ever before, but it's still not enough. We need more volunteers, young and old, who can give a month, six months, or a year of their lives or even more, to helping their brothers and sisters in Appalachia. I assure you, you will gain even more than you give, and you will not regret your sacrifice.

If you know of a person with a good heart and time on their hands, young or old, please tell them to write to us.

We need businesses to relocate in Appalachia. If you are a businessman or businesswoman and you need a new challenge, a new dream to follow, please talk to us. We'll do everything we can to make sure you are successful at the same time that you provide jobs to Appalachia's poor.

We also need businesses to help our Operation Sharing program grow. If you have excess inventory, or "out-of-style" merchandise, you can join in our dreams by letting us put it to good use in Appalachia.

It doesn't take a lot to join in this dream. Every little bit, every little dream counts. When little dreams come true, big dreams grow, and they come true as well.

Whatever your lot in life, we need your help to help make our dreams for Appalachia come true. We need you specifically. We need your unique talents and your resources . . . we need your dreams.

Afterword— Reverend Beiting's Contagious Dreams

By Michael McLaughlin
President of the Christian Appalachian Project

. . . where dreamers lead, and pass the torch to a new generation . . .

This book is about dreams—dreams and faith. It is the story of how a young priest, a hopeless dreamer, worked out his vision among the poor of Appalachia. Now 68 years old, that priest is still a hopeless dreamer—in the most honored sense of that title. His living example of service to others stands as a high beacon to all of us at the Christian Appalachian Project who stand along with him.

Each of the preceding chapters includes dreams for the future, for how will the future be any different from the past without a dream to guide us in a new direction? Dreams are the stars by which we navigate through the sea of our hopes.

I was a senior in college when John Kennedy

said in his inaugural address "the torch has been passed to a new generation of Americans," a generation inspired by its young President to go forth and make war on poverty. I followed his challenge as best as I was able, but by the time I was 34 years of age, the idealism of my youth in that special time in history had worn thin. I needed someone to remind me to dream.

Eighteen years ago I found what I needed in the Christian Appalachian Project and Father Beiting, its inspirational, charismatic leader. In Kentucky I found others whose compassion for the poor was brother and sister to my own. Here was a place where I could learn and grow and serve. Here was fertile ground for dreaming, despite the shallow soil of the mountains.

Here was a priest who could show me Christ's love, not with a sermon on the pulpit, but with a hammer on the roof of an elderly woman's home.

With my energy refocused and my heart rekindled, I began to think again of dreams and aspirations and possibilities.

Father Beiting once told me "Begin each day as if it were a new beginning." I have tried to live that precious bit of advice every day.

He also taught me that, while it was a good thing to have a dream of one's own, it is better by far to dream dreams for others . . . and that the best dreams of all are those that are shared.

The last 18 years have been truly momentous

for me. I have seen CAP grow from a small en-
thusiastic core to a family of over 300 committed
employees, 50 full-time volunteers and hundreds
of part-time volunteers, serving in over a dozen
counties and touching over 40,000 people a year.

Everything that has happened began as a dream
in someone's mind. There has been a lot of trial
and error, misses as well as successes. It has not
been easy, but then we never asked for the road
to be easy, though at times we may have wished
that it were! What we have asked for and received,
are thousands of stars to steer by, those numberless
dreams that are the beginning of each and every
forward movement.

As I reflect on these years, I realize that 18 years
is time enough for a child to be born, to be nurtured by its mother, to move from elementary
school right through high school graduation.

I wonder, have I grown up as well? Have I
graduated? I sense my education is incomplete—I
still have more to learn.

Fortunately for me, my mentor, friend and
leader, that hopeless dreamer, is still around and
active, giving me support—and prodding too when
it is necessary.

All of us at CAP are thankful for Father
Beiting's miraculous constitution, his overall
strength and stamina that has allowed him to survive his accidents and misfortunes of recent years,
to recover and carry on. Eighteen years from now

he will be 86. I can only guess what we will be discussing then . . . but I can guarantee there will be a dream or two involved!

The vision and dream that Father Beiting began is now the legacy of each and every employee, volunteer, and donor of the Christian Appalachian Project. Father Beiting will continue to lead CAP for as long as God gives him the strength, but our noble founder no longer has to carry the dream alone.

His is not a small dream. Even now that the weight of it is shared by the combined shoulders of all of us who came after, it is a heavy load. But for all who share this dream and vision, and who care about those in need, it is a load that is a joy to carry.

We know that every step we take each day, every small action in the name of Jesus, is a mustard seed of dreams and faith that cannot help but change our world forever.

Father Beiting has passed the torch, and our new dreams are the legacy of our leader . . . our hopeless dreamer.

Our bimonthly magazine, *The Mountain Spirit*, will keep you up-to-date on the work of the Christian Appalachian Project as we continue to help the people of this poverty-stricken area help themselves. In the magazine, you will also find moving, inspiring stories about the people we serve. If you would like to subscribe to this publication (or renew your subscription), please complete the order form below.

———————————————————————

THE MOUNTAIN SPIRIT Subscription Order Form

Please enter my one-year subscription to *The Mountain Spirit*. I have enclosed my check for $6.00, made payable to CAP.

Name _____

Address _____

City _____ State _____ Zip _____

Please return this Order Form, along with your check, to: Christian Appalachian Project, 322 Crab Orchard Road, Lancaster, KY 40446.

If You'd Like to
Know More About the
Christian Appalachian Project . . .

For more information about CAP, or for
additional copies of *Dreams of Faith* . . .
please write or phone us at our headquarters:

Christian Appalachian Project
322 Crab Orchard Road
Lancaster, KY 40446
(606) 792-3051

Thank you for your interest and support!